Epiphyte	Terrestrial	Comments
x		Upright stems, variable sizes last for weeks
x		B. digbyana - famous stud plants to make Brassocattleya
x		Spectacular stems unusual spider-like flowers
	x	Attractive flowers - plant doubles in size each year
	x	Flowers when leaves drop
x		Leaves drop before blooming
x		Still king of the orchids
x		Many varieties - hybridized to have varieties bloom in every month
x		Among largest number of orchid varieties and color
x		Akin to Cattleya - blooms more often, smaller but larger number of flowers
x		Famous dancing lady orchids, new fantastic miniatures
	x	Famous Nun's orchid - very easy to grow, blooms last for weeks
x		Fast growing house pot plant blooms for months
x		Vandaceous type - several varieties
x		Recent successes in developing new colors, sizes, and number of flowers per stem
	x	Famous Hawaiian - Vanda - flowers used for leis and store promotions
	x	Source of vanilla bean

*Epiphyte means "plant which grows upon another". These orchids originally grew on trees or rocks and roots seldom touched the ground. Grow in a porous special orchid mix.

**Terrestrials: This group grows in the ground, well-drained soil is recommended.

To Mildred, my wife; Bert, Rodney and Tom, my sons; and their families.

The continuing publication of "Growing Orchids is Fun" is dedicated to A.P. and Mildred Hollingsworth, both of whom passed away in 1996. Their pioneering spirit, dedication and hard work, assisted in laying the foundation for the ever increasing popularity of orchids today.

GROWING ORCHIDS IS **FUN**

- Lighting
- Watering
- Fertilizing
- Blooming

Endorsed by the

AMERICAN ORCHID SOCIETY

www.AOS.org

BETTER-GRO

We Know Orchids · We Grow Orchids

Species & Hybrid Orchids

*Epiphyte (Air Plants) & **Terrestrial Orchids (Grow in Soil)

Kind of Orchid	Usual Time to Bloom	Color	No. Flowers
Ascocentrum	Variable	Yellows, Orange, Red	Many per stem
Brassavola	Spring	Green, Yellow, White	1 or more
Brassia	Spring, Summer	Green, Yellow, Spotted	Several per stem
Bletilla	Spring	Lavender	1-2
	Winter	Lavender-Pink	1-2
Calanthe	Spring	White	Many
Cycnoches and Catasetum	Winter	Green-Yellow	Many
Cattleya	Spring, Summer	Many	1-20
	Winter		
Dendrobium	Spring, Summer	Many	Many
	Winter		
Epidendrum and Encyclia	Spring, Summer	Many	Many
	Winter		
Laelia	Variable	Many	1-10
Oncidium	Spring	Yellow-Red	Many
	Summer, Winter	Brown	
Phaius	Spring	Reddish	10-30
		Yellow-Brown	
Phalaenopsis	Winter	White, Pink	Many
	Spring	Yellow	
Rhynchostylis	Variable	Several	Many
Vanda	Spring	Many	Many
	Summer		
	Winter		
Vanda (Terete)	Spring	Whites to	Many
		Lavenders	
Vanilla	Summer	Greenish	Many
		White	

GROWING ORCHIDS IS FUN

Simple Facts About Growing Orchids

By Albert P. Hollingsworth

1st Edition – May, 1988
2nd Edition – March, 1989
3rd Edition – February, 1990
4th Edition – February, 1991
5th Edition – January, 1992
6th Edition – January, 1993
7th Edition – January, 1994
8th Edition – January, 1995
9th Edition – September, 1995
10th Edition – July, 1996
11th Edition – April, 1997
12th Edition – November, 1997
13th Edition – September, 1998
14th Edition – March, 1999

15th Edition – September, 1999
16th Edition – March, 2000
17th Edition –August, 2000
18th Edition –February, 2001
19th Edition –May, 2001
20th Edition –January, 2002
21st Edition –April, 2002
22nd Edition –January, 2003
23rd Edition –March, 2003
24th Edition –March, 2004
25th Edition –June, 2004
26th Edition –March, 2005
27th Edition –January, 2006
28th Edition –July, 2007

Library of Congress Catalog Card Number: TX 2-449-004
ISBN Number 0-9622279-1-9

Manufactured in United States of America
Sun Bulb Co.
Arcadia, Florida
www.better-grow.com

Preface

Ascda. Jan Hollingsworth

This book is written for beginners, hobbiests and all orchidists as an adventure in the joy of growing orchids. The thrill of walking into your room or yard and seeing the beauty, brilliance and grandeur of orchid blooms coming from a plant far less beautiful can bring the greatest happiness in your life. For the first time you realize that you can grow such a jewel, your enjoyment grows as you add plants and your challenges increase as you see the individuality of varieties, sizes and colors. You will acquire additional living that you never knew existed. I am in no way attempting to introduce a new theory or scientific research. This book is written in everyday terms of easy and practical ways you can apply to growing orchids.

The author acknowledges indebtedness to many whose articles, advice, books, and suggestions have attributed to my success in growing orchids.

My sincerest thanks
to the following:

American Orchid Society
S.R. Batchelor
L.C. Cosper
Frank Fordyce
Tom Harper
Harry B. Logan
Dr. and Mrs. Carlyle A. Luer
Harry Luther
J.R. Moses
Ned Nash
Robert Palmer, III
Mr. and Mrs. John Pelot
Richard Takafuji
Sheldon Takasaki
C.T. Withner

Greg Allikas - ©2006 Photography
Jack of Arts, Inc. - Book Design

Contents

Slc. Jami.Hollingsworth

C. bowringiana

I will always be grateful to Dr. and Mrs. Carlyle A. Luer, Sr., who accounted for my first greenhouses. The Luers had a vision - to collect, preserve and reproduce rare orchid species which they foresaw would become extinct. While their plans were partially developed, Dr. Luer's notoriety and dedication as a surgeon, consumed up to 20 hours each day. Therefore, it became necessary to dispose of his plants and greenhouses in the 1960's. Later in the early 1970's, Dr. Luer retried and about the same time, their dear friend, Mrs. Selby, died. Dr. Luer's position in the bank made it possible to work with the trust officers to carry out Mrs. Selby's wishes for her beautiful home and property located on Sarasota Bay. Their leadership and labor with knowledgeable orchid friends created what has developed into the internationally famous Marie Selby Botanical Gardens.

In recent years, the Luers have traveled world-wide and are presently associated with Missouri Botanical Gardens. Dr. Luer is the author of *The Native Orchids of Florida.*

Albert P. Hollingsworth

Cyrtopodium punctatum

varieties and the *Cattleya bowringiana* bloomed well. Seeing this success my collection grew to other varieties of orchids including potted *Cattleya* hybrids.

As I look into our orchid houses of over a million plants, I wonder, "What would have happened if many years ago my father had not brought the orchid from the Florida cabbage swamps to make peace with my mother for filling her luxurious three-door icebox with wild game?"

When I was a boy, one day my father came home from the Florida Everglades, and on the back seat and floor of his Model T Ford was an eight-point buck deer, a wild bearded turkey gobbler, and from a fallen cypress tree, a strange plant with long sharp horns and hundreds of magnificent tiger spotted yellow-green flowers, a *Cyrtopodium* orchid. The sharp needle pointed horns stuck my finger and it must have infected my life with an incurable disease known as "Orchid Fever".
The symptoms reappeared later in life when I bought a two-horned bulb, a *Bletilla* orchid, planted it in soil and it bloomed a lovely, small cluster of red purple flowers. The burning desire to grow other orchids led me to imported orchids growing on a slab. My blood ran fast as the first bloom was a large green-yellow cattleya-like flower known as a *Brassavola digbyana*. Orchid from British Honduras (Belize), such as *Oncidium*

Your First Orchid

epiphytic orchid; C. mossiae

1. Select a well-grown healthy plant. This is determined by making sure (a) pseudobulbs are firm and plump, (b) leaves are green and firm, (c) roots are firm and healthy.

2. Choose a plant that is easiest to grow in your geographical area.

3. You will want to find a plant that blooms to your preference — lots of small, medium or large flowers.

4. Pick the color you like best. Almost every color is available from shades of lavendar, pastel colors, whites, whites with colored lips, reds, yellows and even greens and blues.

5. Beware of bargains and sickly plants due to disease and dehydration. You learn from experience as your orchid grows. Don't give up! If necessary spend a little extra for a desirable plant. One, perhaps, that is in bud or bloom — giving you instant happiness.

Q. I do not have a greenhouse, can I grow orchids?
A. Yes, many hobbyists grow orchids very successfully on windowsills, patios, or even under trees during warm months.

Q. How long have orchids been grown?
A. History tells us that 2,000 years ago *Cymbidium* orchids were cultivated in Japan and China.

Q. Can I grow orchids?
A. Yes, if you choose orchids you can have a house full of flowers all the time - they will give you color and shapes you never dreamed possible.

Q. What are the secrets of successful growing?
A. There are no secrets; but there are five common sense rules that will determine your success: proper watering, air, light, warmth, and fertilizer.

Q. When do I water my orchids?
A. Let your orchids drink water like you do. When thirsty (dry), water; when wet, leave them alone.

Q. What kind of water should I useto water my orchids?
A. If you can drink it - use it. However, if water source goes through a softener, use water from an outside source that does not go through the "softening" process (which adds considerable sodium.) It is a good idea in any case to flush pots thoroughly with pure water once a month to avoid salt build-up. This is also a good practice if you fertilize your plants regularly. Pure water can be rainwater, distilled water, or well water.

Q. Can I grow orchids in my home?
A. A house that is healthy for you is healthy for orchids.

Q. I do not know anything about growing orchids. How can I keep from killing them?
A. Do not expect instant growth or blooms at first - give an orchid half a chance and it will wait on your education.

Q. Are orchids difficult to grow?
A. Orchids are perhaps the easiest plants to grow and hardest to kill.

SUGGESTED PRONUNCIATIONS

Brussavola	Bra-SAH-voh-la
Brassia	BRASS-ee-a
Cattleya	KAT-lee-a
Cymbidium	Sim-BID-ee-um
Dendrobium	Den-DROH-bee-um
Miltonia	Mil-TOH-nee-a
Oncidium	On-SID-ee-um
Paphiopedilum	Paff-ee-o-PED-ilum
Phalaenopsis	Fal-en-OP-siss
Vanda	VAN-da
Ascocenda	Ass-co-SIN-da
Epidendrum	Eh-pi-DEN-drum

Paph. Maudiae

Monopodial

Monopodial

Characterized by growth of the main stem indefinitely by one main bud in center, grows straight up, wide aerial roots generally grow from where stem and leaf meet. Foliage with thin or thick leathery leaves growing alternately on each side of stem, blooms come from a stem between leaves. These plants need lots of moisture and usually 50% to 70% shade, and generally do well in very warm, lightly shaded conditions. Dry out potting media before rewatering. Some examples are: Vanilla Orchid, *Vanda, Phalaenopsis*. These plants grow constantly and can become quite tall, producing sprays or clusters of many colors and sizes. Large plants often are never out of bloom as new flower stems grow while blooming stem is still pretty.

Sympodial

Sympodial orchids usually have bulbs (storage tanks for water and food) and are uniformly tough. These are the easiest to grow and include the most beautiful orchids. At the end of the season the front bulb ripens and produces flowers. Then begins the new growth known as a "lead" which comes from an "eye" at the bottom of the front bulb. Varieties such as *Cattleya* produce one set of flowers from each growth. Leaves will last for several years and if bulbs with leaves are not severed from the plant, they add much strength to produce strong growth and more beautiful blooms. Examples of sympodials are: *Cattleya, Epidendrum, Dendrobium,* and *Oncidium*.

Sympodial

Epiphytic
Those with all functional roots exposed to air. Roots in pot merely act to anchor plants in position. Although plants in this class are most often found growing on trees, they are not parasitic. They get nutrients from the air and organic matter is washed down on them by rain - typical example: *Phalaenopsis.*

Semi-Epiphytic
Cattleyas and similar plants that develop root systems beneath the surface of the media are in this class. Some roots may still grow out of pot. They need good drainage.

Terrestrial
Roots like garden plants and true soil dwellers in this class. *Bletia, Bletilla,* and *Habenaria* are among the species

Semi-Terrestrial (also known as hemi-epiphytes)
Originally grew in forests with roots anchored in rich, porous leaf mold on the ground. *Cymbidium, Phaius,* and *Paphiopedilum* are in this class.

Terrestrial

Semi-Terrestrial

Epiphytic

Rhynchostylis gigantea 'Banjong' AM/AOS

While there are thousands of orchid names, basically the name is like your own. The first word of an orchid name is the GENUS name, such as *Cattleya*, and compares to your family name such as Jones. The second word is the SPECIES name and it is like your first name such as Albert. Also, orchids often have nicknames. For example:

Rhynchostylis gigantea 'Banjong' AM/AOS

Genus (family) name: Rhynchostylis

Species (first) name: gigantea (always lower case)

Varietal, or cultivar, name (nickname): Banjong (always in single quotes)

Award: AM/AOS

Classifying Orchids

Lc. Mildred Hollingsworth

Among the most and important classification of orchids was Bailey's "Standard Cyclopedia of Horticulture". Many species have been found since the publication and changes have been made. The process of classification is selecting outstanding similarities and placing them into tribes. Differing tribes are divided in genera (pl.), genus (sgl.). The last division is known as species. The genus is capitalized and the species is lower case. An example is *Cattleya skinneri*. However, some of the species have been found so different in color that a varietal name is added such as *Cattleya skinneri alba*. The long horticultural history of orchids has led to "varietal names" such as alba, or vinicolor, or semi-alba, that do not adhere to strict botanical usage. This should present no problem as long as the grower recognizes that the names are in reality popular names that describe - however inaccurately - something in particular about the type.

Hybrid names are capitalized and genus name is in italics. The hybrid, or "grex" name, is capitalized. On page 7 is a list of tribes, the most popular of the genera in each tribe and an example in each tribe that is closely related. Outstanding crosses within the tribe offer prize-winning intergenerics today. An example:

Brassavola X Cattleya =
Brassocattleya (Bc)

Laelia X Cattleya =
Laeliocattleya (Lc)

Classifying Orchids

V. teres v. aureo-labia

It becomes more complicated when up to three or more genera comprise a hybrid, and usually the name of an outstanding orchid person is used with–ara- at the end, such as *Kirchara*. You will understand the value of these methods as even today, new species are often found.

Tribe–The classification of plants forming a subdivision of an order and containing a number of genera.

Genus–A group of related plants consisting of one or more species possessing certain common structural characteristics distinct from those of any other group.

Species–Plants ranking below a genus that have certain permanent characteristics in common.

The method by which over 30,000 orchid species are classified is to first select the general similarities between groups and form several tribes. The orchids were divided into several tribes and orchids with their own characteristics were assigned to individual tribes. For example, take the *Aerides* tribe. The genera that are in this one tribe or family include *Phalaenopsis, Vanda, Aerides,* and many others. While all these genera have similar features, there are differences in the plants and blooms. The most important feature is that genera within the *Aerides* tribe can be cross-pollinated to create intergenerics. The attempt to cross-pollinate plants of two separate tribes has not proven successful.

The following list includes most of the orchid tribes, the orchid genera in the tribe and an example of one of the many species in each genus.

Den. superbum

Classifying Orchids

Tribe	Genus	Example of Species
Aerides	Phalaenopsis	mannii
	Vanda	coerulea
	Aerides	odorata
	Renanthera	storei
	Arachnis	flos-aeris
	Vandopsis	gigantea
	Ascocentrum	miniatum
	Rhynchostylis	coelestis
Cattleya	Epidendrum	*fragrans
	*Some classified as Encyclia	
	Laelia	anceps
	Cattleya	labiata
	Brassavola	nodosa
	Sophronitis	grandiflora
	Schomburgkia	thompsoniana
	Broughtonia	sanguinea
Cymbidium	Cymbidium	finlaysonianum
Cypripedium	Paphiopedilum	concolor
Dendrobium	Dendrobium	nobile
Odontoglossum	Miltonia	regnellii
	Odontoglossum	crispum
	Oncidium	cebolleta
	Brassia	verrucosa
Catasetum	Catasetum	pileatum
	Cycnoches	chlorochilon
	Mormodes	hookeri
Gongora	Gongora	quinquenervis
	Stanhopea	wardii
Phaius	Phaius	tankervilleae
	Bletilla	striata
	Calanthe	vestita
	Bletia	purpurea
Vanilla	Vanilla	planifolia

Six Simple Requirements for Growing Orchids

1. *Air and ventilation*

2. *Lots of sunlight*

3. *Warmth*

4. *Water*

5. *Fertilizer*

6. *Potting*

An overwatered plant

An underwatered plant

Note to the Hobbyist or How to Kill an Orchid

Often a new orchid grower can find the hobby confusing. For example, a new grower took a problem plant to different experts and here are their opinions:

1. *Too much water*

2. *Too dry*

3. *Not enough light*

4. *Too much light*

5. Finally, one expert advised to get rid of the plant. The new grower moved the plant around on the window sill until it found a happy place, watered it like his other orchid, and today it is his best blooming plant.

By explaining the six simple requirements for growing orchids on the following pages, we will acquaint you with the basics. You can adapt your orchids to your similar or most favorable conditions and location.

C. violacea in its habitat

Air

It is best to let your pots of orchids sit a few inches apart to take full advantage of natural air circulation. Movement of air to an orchid plant is like practice was to Paderewski, who once explained that he practiced faithfully every day.
"If I miss one day's practice," he said, "I notice it. If I miss two days, the critics notice it. If I miss three days, the audience notices it."

"Orchids are very special plants with marvelous ranges of form and many beautiful colors."

Orchids are often called air plants and we could believe they have some miraculous mechanism for absorbing food from the air. Like other plants, orchids extract from the air the primary building block - carbon dioxide. Orchids, however, do use carbon dioxide more efficiently than many other plants.

Therefore, the basic requirement to growing good orchids is providing frequent fresh air. Orchid roots need air as well as water. Let your pots become almost dry before the next watering so air can circulate around the roots in dry, porous orchid potting materials. Thus you have additional strength and vigor from your orchid roots.
If stagnant air becomes a problem, place a fan where it will not blow directly on the plant, but will circulate the air in the general area.

Sunlight

Ascda. John DeBiase 'Fuchs Indigo' FCC/AOS

Good quality light is quite important to the growth of an orchid. Overly careful orchid growers are very likely to grow plants in too much shade in an effort to retain "that nice deep green color." While this condition might be an advantage in growing young seedlings, it is not optimal for mature plants. However, protect your plants from direct sunlight during the middle part of the day and during the summer when light and heat are both greater.

It is true that some varieties of orchids such as cattleyas, vandas, dendrobiums, epidendrums and oncidiums will produce more flowers of better quality if they are grown in strong light. However, phalaenopsis, miltonias, phaius and paphiopedilum are known to grow and bloom well in heavier shade.

Perfect growth balance for orchids is determined between the plant, the light it receives, the nutrients it absorbs, and the temperature of air in which it is kept.

Since light is so important it is wise for you to try a variety of locations and different conditions - based, of course, on your initial research or reading on the type of orchid - until the ideal light is determined. For example, at first give them a reasonable and continuous amount of light. Then gradually transfer them to shadier places until the correct light intensity is reached. Orchids will quickly indicate their light preference. Orchid leaves will fade to yellowish or show a burn in too much light, while leaves become deep green in too much shade. Correct light intensity is that which keep the leaves lighter green, hard and leathery.

You will perhaps try your best to get the right balance for your orchids and wind up like the teacher making a trip with a group of children, who stopped for lunch at a restaurant, where one youngster noticed a slot machine and asked what it was. The teacher launched into a lecture on the evils of gambling. To emphasize the futility of getting something for nothing, she said she'd show them what she meant. She marched up to the machine, put in a nickel, pulled the handle — and hit the jackpot.

"As a cut flower, orchid flowers boast unusual shape and colors, adding a distinct class to every bouquet."

Cym. Golden Elf

Warmth

leaves. Cattleyas, phalaenopsis, oncidiums, vandas and epidendrums are warm growing varieties - these are most widely known and are ones that represent elegance, luxury and beauty.

"Perfection is attained by slow degrees; it requires the hand of time..." VOLTAIRE

Orchids grow best in temperatures between 60 and 85 degrees. In other words, grow your orchids at temperatures compatible with your comfort. Orchids can, however, stand short drops down to freezing and heat up to 120 degrees.

While orchids are hardier and more resistant to cold than most tropical plants, you will want to protect them against frost and snow.

If you can maintain temperatures at around 70 degrees during the colder months, photosynthesis and respiration can be carried on. In other words, your plant will continue to grow. Cold slows down growth and the leaves become brittle. Consistently high temperatures can cause rapid, weak, immature growth.

Orchids prefer warmth and sunshine. Give plants all the light tolerated without burning the

Water and Humidity

growing area beyond that which might normally be the case. Misting with a spray bottle is a temporary fix that demands you be at home, while commercially available humidifiers can provide a more uniform solution.

You will have to learn from experience the time and amount of water your orchids need.

Two ways to test whether a plant needs water:

1. Push your finger down along the inside of the pot. If potting material is moist and cool there is enough water. If it is dry and warm - add water.

2. Learn by the weight of the potted orchid: pick up the pot and if it is light the plant usually needs water; if heavy, hold off watering at that particular time.

Many growers soak their plants thoroughly once a week during the growing period (usually late spring to early fall) before midday. During the week, water lightly, keeping the growing medium moist.

Always remember that orchids are more likely to be killed by overwatering, than by an occasional lack of water!

"Not too little or not too much"

Most of us are guilty of using the hose too much. Undoubtedly, we feel if a little water does good, a lot will do extra good and unknowingly damage our orchid plants. We are like the little boy who asked his father, "What is a 'necessary' evil?" "One that we like so much we don't want to abolish it," said the parent. So, if your orchid is dry - water it; if the medium in the pot is damp - leave it alone. Orchids can use more water during warm, sunny months when roots and plants are growing. The danger of overwatering is particularly great during cooler months when there is little plant activity.

Orchids require more humidity than many other plants as they inherit the habits of their parents in the jungle.
Therefore, especially for orchids grown in the home, it is a good idea to raise the humidity in the

Fertilizing

4. Should we fertilize and water both winter and summer?
It is true the plants require considerably less water and fertilizer during the cold, slow growing months. If Rule #2 is followed, lessened frequency of watering will dictate relatively less fertilization. You may also wish to decrease the amount given at any application to one-half strength.

Plants do not like to be "hungry," particularly during and after blooming. The more you fertilize an orchid, the more sunlight an orchid can successfully utilize.

It is always better to get advice from an orchid authority or an orchid book. Be careful about the directions of your doctor or yardman whose mother won a ceramic vase at an orchid show.

The same goes for your choice of orchid fertilizer: Always trust the products of well-known orchid suppliers, such as Better-Gro. More often than not, they use what they supply because they know it works!

These are the fundamentals of orchid culture: humidity, nutrients, protection, air and light. Accept these conditions and plan to grow your orchids to suit these basic needs. Learn everything you can about (a) the conditions your orchids require, (b) the conditions of the location where you want to grow them, and (c) then adapt your watering and other requirements suited to your location.

Orchids in flower are wondrous beyond all other plants.

F ertilizing is necessary to successfully grow spectacular, healthy, blooming plants.

1. Always follow the directions on the container of fertilizer. For example, if directions are to apply one teaspoon per gallon of water, it refers to a very level teaspoon, not an extra measure we are tempted to use to reward that special plant. All of us are guilty of trying to inflict our creations of combinations or alternate practices of fertilizing on our unsuspecting plants.
2. A reliable frequency of fertilizing is "one fertilizing after three waterings." Plants will continue to absorb fertilizer retained in potting medium after each application.
3. For best results, fertilize your plants immediately after watering or when potting materials are moist. It is best not to fertilize during hottest part of day if plants are warm.

Why do orchids require a special potting media? Let's go back to the native trees, rocks, and conditions where orchids were first found in Central and South America, as well as in tropical Asia. There, orchids are found growing on tree branches. The roots are deep into the crevices of the bark on the limbs, some roots meandering down into the mosses nestled in the bark. Others are just clinging to open limbs. There the plants and roots are exposed to both wet and dry periods, with nutrients from dust and bird droppings seeping down the limbs.

When orchids are potted, wouldn't it be wise to adapt the same conditions? Thus various media used for potting orchids should be of a very porous nature and with good moisture retention. When potted, the porous nature of the media will allow roots aeration and good drainage, and yet hold water and keep roots moist. You may wish to develop your own potting program or choose the media best suited to your plant or plants. You can develop your own mix by choosing materials like graded bark, charcoal, vermiculite, or anything non-toxic that creates a porous mix. Very clean grades of sphagnum from New Zealand and Chile are commonly used for some types of orchids and orchids grown in cedar, teak, or wood baskets. Better-Gro orchid mixes and Better Gro Orchid Moss may be your best option, as these are already formulated and pre-mixed by orchid experts.

As an illustrative example, well-grown *Cattleya* orchids usually send roots directly into porous media. On the other hand, *Phalaenopsis* and *Vandas* will more likely send the roots seeking more aeration than cattleyas. The secret is to observe your plants, learn their habits, water when it is needed, and develop your own potting programs.

Slat Baskets

Clay flowerpots with basal slats on side and hole in bottom

Plastic pots with adequate drainage holes

Label for name should accompany and identify each plant

1. Rhizome pot clip.
2. Stake clamps easily to side of pot. Covered wire recommended to attach to stake, tie around each individual pseudobulb to support plant from shifting when moving or when air circulates.
3. Pot hanger clamps to side of pot if you wish to hang plant.
4. S-hook or extender to add length to pot hanger.

Potting is one of the most important operations in successful orchid growing. While orchids can be repotted anytime during the year, the best time to repot orchids, particularly cattleyas, is immediately after blooming and immediately before new roots and growth begins. Do not overpot, as plant usually stays too wet. Divide plant behind fourth pseudobulb and trim dead roots at bottom of base - leaving as many live white roots as possible. A good rule of thumb is to never divide a plant of less than six strong bulbs.

Select a pot that will accommodate the plant **(1)** and allow 1 1/2 " for new growth (about two years growth). Fill it 1/3 with broken flowerpots, stones or styrofoam peanuts for drainage.

(2). You will want a minimum of three or four good pseudobulbs if you divide a plant.

After the plant has been cleaned and trimmed, hold back bulbs against rim of pot.Hold plant upright and place potting material around roots **(3)** with the rhizome on surface of the materials. Best results are obtained when the rhizome is kept level with the surface of the mix.

You may wish to add more materials around the edge and pack firmly so no pockets are left in the materials and you may wish to put pot clip on rhizome **(4)**. Use pot stake by the side of the plant and tie bulbs with covered wire to stabilize plant from moving until new roots fully support the plant in the pot. A label identifying the name can be tied to the stake or buried securely along inside of pot.

Phalaenopsis - Need to be repotted in early summer if the potting material has rotted and if plant has outgrown its container. Phals are epiphytic and most of the roots are usually outside of the pot and hanging in the air.

Dendrobiums, Laelias, Oncidiums - Vigorous growers and favorites of amateur growers, may be allowed to grow to sizeable plants with 10 or more growths with good results.

DIVIDING

Orchids are best divided when the plant has outgrown the pot. Cattleyas and dendrobiums in particular are usually separated and repotted in smaller pots when plants can be split into two or more four pseudobulb divisions. The front division is the newest portion of the plant. Back bulbs are those from which the front division is separated.
Caution: For continued flowering in shortest time, a separated plant should not be less than three or four pseudobulbs.

However, you may wish to repot entire plant into a larger container and allow it to grow into a sizeable plant. Several lead growths with many flowers at one time, beautifully presented, produce what is known as an exhibition, or specimen, plant.

AIR LAYERING & TOP CUTTING

Vandas and other monopodial genera are "divided" or increased by air layering. A cut is made part way into the stem several inches below top of the plant, if possible below one or two aerial roots. Wrap a ball of sphagnum moss around the cut area and tie securely with a thread or wire. This process should always be done in early summer when new root growth begins. You must keep ball damp at all times. When new roots have grown through the ball, the plant is cut off and potted as a new plant. The original plant should then break with new growth or growths. Alternately, plants with abundant root growth can be top cut through the stem at a point below 4-5 healthy, active roots. Dress both cut parts with fungicide powder and pot top cutting normally in a basket.

Den. chrysotoxum

Dendrobiums are famous for producing offsets from the joints of mature canes. However, Vandaceous type plants frequently also send out offsets. When offset shows adequate roots, carefully cut the plant from the cane and pot as a new plant.

Phalaenopsis also produce offsets, or keikis (Hawaiian for "baby") from the nodes of older flower stems. These offshoots are identical to the mother plant and are an outstanding method of propagating a type that cannot otherwise be easily divided. When the keiki produces two or three leaves and begins to form roots, the young plant can be broken off and potted as for a young seedling. From a stem of *Phalaenopsis* flowers, often an offshoot with a similar plant sprouts from a joint. Also available today is a formulated paste that can be applied to the joints of a *Phalaenopsis* or *Phaius* flowering stem that will force growth of keikis. Cutting a mature, flowered stem and laying on a well-drained soil easily propagate Phaius plants. If kept damp, new plants will grow from the joints.

The futuristic world of biotechnology is seen today in tissue culture or cloning of plants. Reproduction of exact replicas of high quality, very desirable plants, including orchids, takes place in laboratories under sterile conditions. All operations are performed with surgical gloves, masks, disinfectants and special techniques together known as micropropagation, cloning or tissue culture. Superior plants are multiplied by taking a piece of sterilized tissue (usually from the newly emerging growth), placing it in a test tube containing especially formulated nutrients and hormones, and suspending it on a wheel to allow continual bathing of the meristemmatic cells in fresh solution. The process of reproduction has been started. There are several more manipulations to take place before the tissue becomes a plant.

The advantage of meristemming is that uniquely superior plants can be reproduced in large numbers that will grow and bloom identically to the mother plant. Previously, orchid growers had to rely on divisions to increase the stock of particularly good plants. Meristemming has made it possible to distribute highly superior plants - awarded or otherwise - in a surprisingly short time and at very reasonable prices. An additional advantage to the meristem process is that plants with uniformly high quality can be reproduced for distribution, enabling growers and consumer alike to enjoy plants that might have otherwise been restricted to the privileged few.

slab. The size slab usually depends on the size plant you wish to mount. Sometimes a chunk of sphagnum moss or tree fern is placed between the plant's rhizome and the slab. Use only coated wire, string or tape to tie the plant securely to the slab. The sphagnum moss or tree fern acts as a cushion between new roots and slab, as well as retaining moisture to encourage new roots to grow. Slabs dry out quicker than pots and more regular misting and water is necessary.

Epidendrums, oncidiums, species cattleyas, pendulous dendrobiums and other species and botanical orchids grow and bloom well mounted on a slab. Also, a lot of original designs are created when orchids are mounted on driftwood, cypress knees, and other decorative materials and used for indoor or poolside designing. Cypress slabs, particularly the ones with bark on the outside as well as other hardwoods and pieces of cork oak bark are used extensively and many botanicals and species will easily send roots and attach themselves to the

T he technique of cross-pollinating or self-pollinating an orchid is very simple and you can easily make your own crosses. The column containing the reproductive organs is located at base of the labellum or throat of the orchid bloom.

1. With a pointed stick or sharp forceps detach the anther holding the pollinia (pollen) at the tip of the column. Separate the pollinia from the anther.

2. Directly below the anther is a little pocket, usually very sticky, known as the stigmatic surface. With the end of the stick or forceps, transfer the pollen to the sticky pocket and pollination is complete. After pollination the flower wilts and the ovary will enlarge.

3. If the cross is successful, the ovary will enlarge into a seed capsule, which requires from nine to 14 months to mature.

4. The seedpod should be removed when it turns yellow. Do not wait until seedpod cracks and seed is exposed.

5. Orchid seed is sown in bottles of special nutrient jelly within a sterile laboratory or planting cage. Sterile precautions should be taken the entire time the seeds are growing. If mold appears on the jelly, it must be removed or it will kill all the young plants. Few people have special equipment to sow orchid seed but there are many laboratories that will accept and flask your seed. Within a year the seeds will develop into little orchid plants.

6. Most growers transplant 15 to 25 plantlets into a 3" pot filled with fiber or orchid potting mix, known as a community pot. Be sure the plants have developed about 1/2 inch roots before opening and removing from the flask. Plants in the community pots should be kept moist and carefully watched daily for signs of fungus. This is usually indicated by leaves turning black. It is best to drench the plants with a mild fungicide every few days after planting from the flask.

7. When plants have overgrown the compot (about 1" high or larger) transplant to small individual 2" pots. In about a year the 2" pot seedling should have grown large enough to transfer to 3" or 4" pot. Do not overpot. Your plants are now growing well and can eventually be repotted to 4" to 6" pots to develop into blooming size plants.

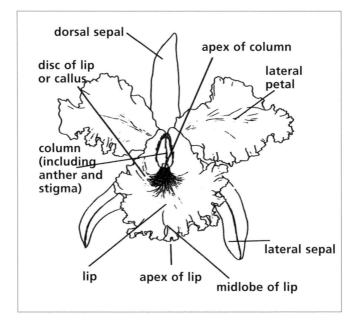

dorsal sepal

apex of column

disc of lip or callus

lateral petal

column (including anther and stigma)

lip

apex of lip

midlobe of lip

lateral sepal

An assortment of colorful Cattleya hybrids

Cattleya

Like diamonds with their grandeur in so many shapes, sizes, sparkle and beauty.

C. gaskelliana

Cattleyas excel with the greatest charm and challenge of all orchids! Untamed, cattleyas run wild and explode in the greatest variety of colors and exotic shapes ever seen in orchids, bursting out with one to 100 blooms at a time! Describing cattleyas is like trying to describe the heavens. There are crosses that bloom in spring or summer or fall or winter - so with a few plants you have loads of orchids every day; and some will thrill you all day with alluring fragrance.

Hybridizing with related genera such as *Laelia, Brassavola, Sophronitis* and *Epidendrum* has expanded cattleyas, as a type. The hybrids can bloom several times a year; producing a rainbow of color; they are more compact; easier to grow; and mature quicker. They offer everything you would want in an orchid! Purple cattleyas once held the title of "Miss Orchid." Perhaps they are still the "mind's eye" picture of an orchid to many. However, in recent years, the hybridist's art has yielded a large number of colors, shapes and combinations that never cease to fascinate. Where do these man-made hybrids come from, with their outstanding vigor, single flowered or in clusters with full, circular blossoms and gigantic fringed lips? One can only wonder and be grateful that, more importantly, all these are widely available at reasonable prices. The genera that have been widely intercrossed to produce bigeneric crosses as *Brassocattleya* and trigeneric crosses like *Brassolaeliocattleya* are as follows:

Laelia introduces a great variety of color, longer pseudobulbs, and, often, larger blooms. You can pick a variety for spring, summer, fall, and winter. Two species, *Laelia rubescens* and *Laelia anceps* are easy to grow and bloom. These two are highly recommended for beginners. Another wonderful plant for beginners, particularly in frost-free areas, is *Laelia purpurata*, the national flower of Brazil. Robust plants up to 24" or more bear a profusion of large flowers right around Mother's Day. The rupicolous types need to be kept very dry and in bright light. Laelias are noted and popular, particularly for the following characteristics:

1. May bloom two or more times per year.
2. Bifoliate (two leaves per pseudobulb) producing most vigorous hybrids.

3. Accounts for new colors in deep bronzes, clear yellows, glowing pinks and lavenders.
4. From five to 25 good sized, waxy-lipped flowers per stem of corsage white flowers.
5. Small miniature varieties as well as large standards.

Sophronitis coccinea endows its offspring with deep, brilliant red colored flowers on short, compact plants. While originally from higher elevations and cool growing, many of its hybrids easily adapt to warmer   climates. This species is the greatest influence in creating minicatts by combining brilliant red, orange and yellow colors. They are vigorous growers and prolific bloomers.

Broughtonia sanguinea has introduced clear red, pink and white flowers from warm growing plants that will tolerate full sun. These include famous miniature hybrids bearing many breathtaking flowers. Especially the waxy reds, with very good form and excellent texture, can be known as the orchid of the future. Many have called this gem the "Ruby" of all orchids.

B. nodosa

Rhyncholaelia digbyana has ruled orchid breeding for over 100 years. Its vigorous stamina brings giant blooms with large fuzzy lips particularly in greens, yellows, pinks and lavenders. If you see a healthy plant with this parent - GET IT! You will be especially enthralled by the penetrating and exotic lemony fragrance that is so strong after dark.

Brassavola nodosa is known as the "Dama de la noche" - with this reputation every collector should seek this orchid famous for its heavy fragrance after dusk and large unusual heart-shaped white lip. The unbelievable vigor produces spectacular specimen plants covered with loads of blooms.

The most beautiful orchids in the world are cattleyas. Hobbyists can grow more different kinds of cattleyas than any other orchid and the plants and flowers are enjoyed in all seasons. Their many different sizes, shapes, colors and fragrances continue to increase their popularity. You will be interested in some of the species, originally found in jungles of Central and South America, which are responsible for the spectacular

Rhynch. digbyana

The First Cattleya

Blc. Pamela Hetherington 'Coronation' FCC/AOS

hybrids available today. Most species are fragrant. Some of the species such as *Cattleya dowiana* are almost impossible to find in the jungle today. CITES (The Convention on International Trade in Endangered Species) has restricted many countries from shipping out wild collected species plants, however, many new nurseries in the range states are propagating their native species for sale to waiting customers.

Some species are available, but you may find the plants more costly than a beautiful hybrid. Several growers have reproduced species by meristem methods, so if you must grow species cattleyas, keep asking and looking and you will be rewarded. *Laelia, Cattleya* and *Brassavola* are the top three most important genera, and these have been primarily used in the development of hybrids. The following varieties will become familiar to you as they are the majority grown today or have been used in hybridizing.

The First Cattleya

Many believe in Lady Luck, and we could say that the discovery of

the first *Cattleya* was luck. In 1818 a collection of mosses were tied together with some thick leafed, long bulb plants and shipped to England. When the material arrived, a horticulturist was curious about the plants used for packing, as they were different from any he had ever seen. When the plant bloomed, it was found to be truly different and a new genus was recorded as *Cattleya* (named *Cattleya labiata autumnalis* after the grower, William Cattley; the showy lip of the flower; and the season of bloom). Today, we still thrill to the lavender pink flowers with a beautiful lip that bloom in the fall. The publicity of this new discovery spread over Europe and many collectors rushed to collect additional plants. While they spent years in the jungle, they never found the location of the original native plant. The search continued and during the next 20 years *Cattleya mossiae, Cattleya gigas (warscewiczii)* and *Cattleya trianaei* were discovered and sent to England. Also about that time *Cattleya dowiana* was found in Costa Rica. Because of the spectacular large showy flowers these four species became the greatest breeding plants for the development of famous hybrids.

The plants along with other unifoliate species were so similar to *Cattleya labiata*; they were considered varieties of that species and named *C. labiata* variety mossiae, etc. Today, however, the plants are known as separate species such as *C. mossiae*. Because the other group of similar species had two to three leaves instead of one leaf per pseudobulb, they are known as "bifoliate."

C. mossiae

The Heritage of Cattleya Species

Modern orchid growers have become so accustomed to the results of nearly 150 years of hybridizing that the charm and elegance of species is becoming increasingly in demand and highly sought-after. Growers in the Latin American countries from which the species progenitors of our modern hybrids originate have long selected and propagated the very finest examples of their native species. So, as demand for good *Cattleya* species increases, so does supply from both offshore and domestic growers. Not only are select strains of *Cattleya* alliance species more available and of higher quality than any time in the past, but astute breeders are using them to recreate long-lost primary (species x species) and near primary (species x hybrid) hybrids of wonderful exuberance and in a riot of colors and fragrances. Don't overlook the hybrid vigor added when species are used in hybridizing.

The Labiate Group (unifoliate)
Cattleya mossiae

Early fame came to this species when it bloomed at Easter and Mother's Day. Flowers up to 8" in diameter, the bloom is deep rose-lavender in color with wide ruffled petals, yellow, purple striped throat and three to four or more flowers per stem. Other varieties were also found such as var. *reineckiana*, a white with a purple throat. Var. *wageneri*, white with yellow throat, has been very important in hybridizing and producing the best corsage whites.

Cattleya trianaei

Equally as important as *C. mossiae*, it blooms during December and January and it delights orchid growers with Christmas flowers. The flowers are about 7" wide and there are a large number of various colors - pinkish-lavenders to crimson. Also several white forms of *C. trianaei* were discovered and have been successfully grown. The flowers have very broad petals and a long lip with a yellow throat. The blooming period can often start in autumn and some varieties bloom into March. Therefore, *C. trianaei* is a very versatile and important plant and has produced famous hybrids to bloom during six separate months of the year. Also *C. trianaei* is famous for growing rapidly into spectacular specimen plants.

C. dowiana

Cattleya dowiana

No yellow colored orchid has yet to reach the many years of popularity of the large yellow *Cattleya dowiana* with large purple, wide-lip, lined with gold. It was the first yellow *cattleya* discovered and still today many hybrid yellow orchids owe the brilliance of color and hard texture to its original dowiana background. For example, *C. dowiana* can be discovered as one of the species in the parentage of both *Lc.* Bonanza and *Blc.* Norman's Bay. Sadly, this fine species is not always the easiest plant to grow well, and cultivars with good quality blooms are rare, expensive and highly sought-after.

Cattleya aurea

Discovered in Colombia, it has individualized itself from the Costa Rican *C. dowiana* and is considered by some to be a separate species, especially owing to the much different results obtained when is it used in hybridizing. It is a much larger plant and the flowers are deeper yellow, the lip is more heavily marked with gold and some plants produce flowers with red markings. *Cattleya aurea* is known to produce many gorgeous flowers of richly varied colors when hybridized with other cattleya species.

Cattleya warscewiczii

Also known as *C. gigas*. The largest of all cattleya species, its blooms can reach 10" in diameter with up to seven flowers per stem. Flowers are rosy-lavender with an extra wide reddish ruffled lip, and marked with yellow "eyes." Growers in the south and where night temperatures are warm may find this species difficult to bloom.

Cattleya luteola

This "minicatt" species has clusters of small yellow flowers with or without purple on the lip. A native of Brazil it usually blooms during winter months. As one of the parents of the famous *Sc.* Beaufort (x *Soph. coccinea*), *C. luteola* is responsible for some of the finest dwarf and compact catt-leya hybrids yet seen, in a sparkling array of yellow, oranges, reds and related shades.

C. warscewiczii

C. maxima

Cattleya percivaliana

A Christmas orchid with several dainty rose flowers that bear colorful frilled lips, with the throat showing colors of orange, violet and maroon. The growth habit and flower size is very comparable to a one half scale *C. labiata*. Despite it's strong perfume that some do not like, it has proven to be an important parent of compact growing standard cattleyas for the winter season.

C. luteola

Cattleya maxima

A very popular large light lavender rose flower that was discovered in the early 1900's. The slender flowers lack quality required for large popular compact flowers and for many years grown in only a few collections. Today, this species is gaining popularity not for the individual blooms, but for the sensational display given of several heads of the colorful blooms on well-grown plants.

Cattleya gaskelliana

One of the easiest cattleyas to grow and it bears nicely shaped violet flowers suffused with white in the early summer. The lip is large deep purple and a yellow streaked throat. The white variety, alba, has a crimson lip.

C. aurantiaca

The Bifoliate Group

The bifoliate group of cattleyas is very different than the *C. labiata* type and has rapidly become popular for use in hybridizing. So-called because there are two to three leaves on each pseudobulb. The pseudobulbs are often quite thin compared to the *C. labiata* type, and can be anywhere from 4" (in *C. aclandiae*) to 60" (in *C. guttata*.) The flowers are smaller, many are waxy, and grow in clusters up to 30 flowers per stem. The lip is narrow and pointed, often differently shaped and properly described as a "spade" lip. The greatest advantage of bifoliates is that they have bloomed in so many colors and combinations of colors. Several flowers have lips that are a completely different color from the flower petals. Colors, spotting and markings include lavenders, pinks, orange, yellow, green, brown, reddish, white, and blue. Because bifoliate flowers are smaller than the

C. labiata group, they were less popular for a long time as people prefer big, showy flowers. Through the years the results of cross breeding the two types of orchids produced an ideal medium-size flower, many blooms per plant, and a fantastic array of colors. Today the bifoliate and *C. labiata* types are equally popular and have produced many spectacular hybrids. Here are a few of the bifoliate species that are easily available and are grown by many hobbyists.

Cattleya aurantiaca

This species produces a small, dainty cluster of deep orange flowers usually blooming on 3"-15" long pseudobulbs. While collectors are still able to gather these plants from the jungles, perhaps saving the orchids from destruction by land developers, it is the highly inbred, select forms that are most often seen. These flowers can range from deepest orange-red through yellow to near white. *C. aurantiaca* is best known for its influence in making red, cluster type orchids.

C. aclandiae

Cattleya bowringiana

Fifty years ago you would have found this cattleya in every orchid collection as large quantities of plants at low prices were shipped out of Belize (then known as British Honduras). Up to 30 rose purple 3" flowers bloom from a 12" to 24" cylindrical pseudobulb which is recognized by a round egg-like "bulb" at the base. The intense colors and increased number of flowers resulting from crossing this species with *C. labiata* types has produced important hybrids. Some growers were very lucky when they bloomed a blue flower variety. This is a popular and important parent in the development of blue cattleya hybrids. DNA Research has shown that the Central American species, *C. bowringiana*, *C. skinneri*, *C. aurantiaca* and *C. deckeri*, and a few related species, have enough differences from the South American cattleyas to place them in their own genus, *Guarianthe*. However, you will still find them offered for sale as cattleyas.

C. bowringiana

everyone loved the sparkling 31/2" rose purple flowers that lasted for weeks. A plant that easily grows mounted on a slab as well as in a pot. Specimen plants are a sight to behold. Also there is a pure white form. *C. skinneri* is the national flower of Costa Rica. The natives use the plants for bouquets, to decorate the inside and outside of their homes, to place on the altar and as floral decorations in parades.

Cattleya deckeri

Commonly known as a fall blooming *C. skinneri* var. *autumnalis*. Very similar, of course, but with somewhat shorter, fatter pseudobulbs and fuller shaped blooms.

Cattleya violacea

Also known as *C. superba*, *C. violacea* is an important orchid in the development of novelty hybrids. The 5" round, flat, deep rose petals and a deep crimson well-shaped yellow lip, streaked with purple that blooms in the spring. This is not always the easiest species to grow well.

C. skinneri

Cattleya skinneri

This orchid was shipped out of Costa Rica in large quantities as

The Heritage of Cattleya Species

C. intermedia v. aquinii

amethyst color that is also predominant on the lip. These colors have been easily transferred into hybrids and the species, *C. intermedia* aquinii continues today as a popular stud plant.

Cattleya walkeriana

This species originates in an area of Brazil that has a definite wet and dry season. This can present a problem to some who try to grow the species, which does not flower unless a dry winter season is observed. The flowers are pinkish

Cattleya intermedia

Blooms are held in clusters of four to five pink to milky 5" flowers with narrow petals and an amethyst colored, tubular lip with a ruffled edge. The plants produce 18" pseudobulbs. There is also an alba or white form.

Cattleya intermedia var. aquinii

A famous and important orchid that is responsible for gorgeous "splashed" petal *Cattleya* hybrids. The broad ruffled white petals are marked with patches of rich

C. walkeriana

lavender, good texture and fragrant. *C. walkeriana* has become one of the most important breeders of new, compact cattleya hybrids. An important characteristic is that, when crossed with a large flowered species or hybrid, the hybrid's flowers remain relatively large, while the plants are quite compact.

Cattleya schilleriana

A most important species in the development of hybrids as its olive green, tinted brown, and dark purple spots colors have been used to intensify green coloring and spotting in hybrid cattleyas.

C. walkeriana v. alba

Cattleya aclandiae

Crossing to get better yellows and greens as well as spots, *C. aclandiae* has made its place in the early history of hybrids. The plant can be difficult to grow, although seed-raised populations are becoming more available and seem to be easier to maintain in cultivation.

C. leopoldii

C. amethystoglossa

Cattleya amethystoglossa

The predominant feature of this orchid is the many pearly pink, rose spotted blooms borne in striking clusters on erect inflorescences above 30"+ pseudobulbs. This gem is for those who like many medium size blooms.

Cattleya elongata

A tough, easy to grow orchid that will endure growing dry and will tolerate stronger sunlight. 12" canes produce clusters of waxy, fragrant 3 1/2" red flowers with purple lips.

Cattleya forbesii

Because of the yellow-green color this species is used by some wishing to develop better yellow hybrids. However, the flowers are smaller and do not have the flat form which hybridizers are seeking. While many might easily pass over this compact species owing to it rather nondescript (often described as "tan") flowers, others find that it has an indescribable "something" that draws their attention.

Cattleya guttata

Many hybrids are derived from the many different color forms of this spectacular species. Colors include yellow and green, many with predominate fine spotting, and some with a particular chestnut color. The growth, size of blooms, and flower clusters are very similar to *C. amethystoglossa*.

Cattleya leopoldii

A robust grower, often confused with *C. guttata*, with mahogany sepals and petals spotted with crimson, and a rose-purple lip.

L. anceps

Cattleya granulosa

This is another species of special value to hybridizers of green orchids. Up to nine flowers on one stem, the 4" olive green, sometimes spotted, flowers have readily attracted hybridizers. The flowers are waxy and the spear shaped lip is yellow to rose.

Cattleyas and laelias are commonly found growing in Central and South America. However, not all of the species grow in one particular area. They are found in trees or on rocks at high and low altitudes. When one considers the variety of habitats from which these many and varied species originate, you will understand why plants easily grow when the best conditions are found. The difference between the two are: *Laelia* has eight pollinia; *Cattleya* structure shows four pollinia while *Laelia* flowers are smaller than cattleyas. Their greatest contribution to hybrids are the brilliant colors of scarlet, yellow,

orange, bronze, and blue. While crossing cattleyas with laelias, *Cattleya* contributes the shape and large size while the distinct coloring comes from laelias.

Laelia anceps

Large showy 4" lavender flowers bloom from tall arching stems with several flowers lasting seven or eight weeks. A very easy plant to grow in pots or mounted on a slab. For many years thousands of these plants were brought out of Mexico and perhaps *L. anceps* were always included in the collection of every orchidist. Today, most plants are divisions of these original importations, or are raised from seed or tissue culture. *L. anceps* is very popular as a Thanksgiving and Christmas orchid.

Laelia rubescens

Vigorous growing fall bloomers that can be grown mounted, in pots or in baskets for specimen plants. A cluster of eight lavender and blue, blush to pure white flowers bloom from an arching 12" stem.

Laelia purpurata

The national flower of Brazil, *Laelia purpurata* is a real collectors favorite. This beautiful species has produced flowers with so many shades of rose-purple, purple, blue and reddish. The 8" flowers and bell-shaped lip with intense color has been used by more hybridizers than many other laelias.

L. purpurata v. purpurata

L. purpurata blooms at Mother's Day in the Northern Hemisphere and is very popular as a decorative plant at that time. Scientists have transferred most of these laelias from Brazil into the genus *Sophronitis*. It is likely however, that commercially they will continue to be called *Laelia* for some time to come.

Laelia tenebrosa

The flowers are very similar to L. purpurata but the flowers are bronze to yellow. The 8" wide flowers with unusual color has accounted for the species popularity.

Laelia crispa

A popular summer flower whose blooms are large, fragrant, with ruffled petals and lips. It is a good white with purple lip and was one of the first of the genus to be crossed with *Cattleya* to form an early bigeneric hybrid.

Laelia xanthina

Another collector's favorite that has attracted many hybridizers of yellow orchids. Another good yellow stud plant which blooms 3-inch clear yellow flowers, a yellow lip veined red-purple.

Laelia flava

A hybridizer's choice selection for yellow hybrids as the species plant will bloom with eight or more bright yellow 2 1/2" blooms on a 12" spike. The strong yellow color makes it a favorite of many orchid growers.

Laelia harpophylla

This species is famous for the quantity of scarlet orange flowers with a ruffled lip. *L. harpophylla* is an important background species in the production of brilliant winter flowering cluster type cattleyas.

Laelia cinnabarina

Easily confused with *L. harpophyllia* but the flowers are red-orange. The spikes are erect, 12"-24" long with up to 15 flowers.

Laelia pumila

Four-inch rose flowers with wide rose petals, long reddish purple lip, which blooms from a short, dwarf pseudobulb.

Mini-cats for the multitudes - small but mighty - a new trend in orchids beginning in the 50's, accelerating through the 90's and continuing today has exposed thousands of growers to the beauty of cattleyas. You will find in these the BEAUTY SECRETS of orchids. Everything you will want in an orchid such as:

Lc. Mini Purple 'Blue Hawaii' AM/A

1. Grows easily in every area of the country.
2. The compact plants require much less space - a boon to "cramped quarters".
3. If grown slightly damp with constant humidity and light potting material to keep roots airy, the plants will thrives in the medium to bright light common in homes. Leaves like to be kept relatively cool.
4. Pick a hybrid that produces your favorite color, as mini-cats are all colors and endless combinations.
5. Some crosses start blooming two to three years quicker from seedlings than most orchids and more important, in smaller pots. Faster growing to bring a glorious array of flowers. Look for new introductions that will feature more famous and beautiful orchids in the future. Every day there is something new to enjoy about growing orchids. It has been said that experience is the stuff that when you finally get enough of, you're too old to qualify for the job.

The Orchid, by "Nos Vemos"

It caught my eye as I was driving by
So that instinctively I braked to look,
Amazed at such a mass array of bloom
The colored front page of a florist's book.

Solid purple for two feet long or three,
One great unbroken rank of blazing flower,
My heart leapt as it looked maybe to me,
They could be orchids filling up that bower.

On the Verandah now I could go near,
They were so lovely but my head was clear
I would come again favor mañana
It was Cattleya bowringiana.

Cattleyas

Pot. Twentyfour Carat `Lea' AM/AOS

Otra. Hwa Yuan Bay 'She Shu'

Lc. Orglade's Paradise 'MGR' HCC/AOS

Lc. Christopher Gubler 'Betty's Beau' AM/AOS

Lc. Trick or Treat

Blc. Hawaiian Passion 'Carmela' HCC/AOS

Blc. Red Passion

Blc. George King 'Serendipity' AM/AOS

Encyclias & Epidendrums

Encyclia cordigera

Enc. tampensis

(Epidendrum means "upon trees")

Just try and keep encyclias and epidendrums from growing! They are tough and prolific and can stand more abuse than just about any orchid. These vigorous orchids are found in hammocks and swamps all over Florida. *Epi. magnoliae* grows in trees from South Carolina to Louisiana and throughout Florida. While these plants were considered pests in trees many years ago, it is becoming nearly impossible to locate plants today. And it is rare indeed to find specimen plants as big as a wash tub that at one time were plentiful. Some deer and wild turkey hunters and orchid collectors have even lucked upon Alba varieties of *Enc. tampensis*. Some areas in which *Epi. magnoliae* were found have winters below freezing and much work is being done to hybridize them with warm blooded

cattleyas, laelias and brassavolas to expand hardy traits into warm growing varieties. Growers like encyclias and epidendrums for the bright colors, dependable blooms (every year) and large number of stems per plant. Over 1000 varieties have been found from the United States, throughout Mexico, Central America and mountain ranges of South America. Less than 100 varieties are regularly seen with flowers from 1" to 3" wide. Today orchidists divide the genus into two categories. *Encyclia* mostly identifies the egg-shaped pseudobulb varieties that thrive indoors or in protected areas outdoors. The name *Epidendrum* applies to other varieties more commonly known as "reedstems." The distinction was more obvious in simpler times, and today, taxonomists are trying to make sense of this large and diverse group of orchids. Unfortunately for growers, what makes sense to a taxonomist - those who decide the "proper" names for orchid species - doesn't always seem clear to the horticulturist.

Pot or slab epidendrums and grow in same conditions as cattleyas; generally epidendrums can survive more light and heat. About the only way to kill the plant is keeping it saturated with water, high burning heat or freezing. Most plants have rich perfumes and *Enc. alata* has been known to leave its fragrance in a room for days. Several popular varieties are easily available at a price to suit your pocketbook. There is *Enc. atropurpureum* (aka *Enc. cordigera*) which when blooming with rose lip known as *roseum* and

Enc. cordigera

another type with a white lip with 2 rose stripes that it is called randii. Other available favorites are *Enc. alata, Enc. phoenicia, Enc. gracilis* and the Florida native, *Enc. tampensis. Epidendrum obrieanum*, first known as a "weed" is the most popular reed stem variety and it will produce large orange-red clusters of flowers all year. As fast as old ones wither and drop off, new flowers come out. The most common reedstem type is known as *Epi. ibaguense*, however, you may also find the plants labeled *Epi. radicans*. Radicans usually have short bamboo thin stems and colors range from red, yellow, lavender to white. On Miami Beach and Hawaii these epidendrums are used in land-scaping and plants grow in dense and twining masses - a sight to behold. The stems are leafy and have aerial roots to cling and support each other. These can grow in tem-peratures up to 105°. The plants grow equally well in pots and thrive where there is heavy light and warmth.

You can also grow *Epi. radicans* and *Epi. ibaguense* (as well as their many, many hybrids!) in your yard in full sun beds. A most popular reed stem species, Epi. pseudepidendrum is noted for their bright green petals and scarlet orange lip. Recently hybrids from using this as a stud plant have received high recognition for many brilliant green and deep orange flowers growing from plants up to 6' tall.

You will love epidendrums as they have been known to bloom 500 flowers at a time from one plant and reed stem flowers are a knockout in arrangements. If you are just beginning to grow orchids, you will gain confidence and learn a lot from epidendrum plants.

In the history of orchids, *Encyclia cochleata*, botanically known as *Prosthechea cochleata*, was the first epiphytic orchid to bloom in England. While many epidendrums have con-tributed to the creation of famous hybrids, there are only a few species and botanicals still easily available at a reasonable cost. Some varieties are still imported from a few Central American countries. Several species are being "selfed and seeded". The plants will show up for sale at orchid shows and in orchid advertise-ments from time to time. Therefore, there is a good possibility of getting varieties that are described below. Some examples of both encyclias and epidendrums are listed on the following pages.

Encyclias & Epidendrums

Enc. alata

Encyclia alata

Most popular for its fragrance. The flowers are yellow with traces of purple and it blooms in the spring on an arching stem. It's rare and the outstanding big brother has a much larger flower with the same color and fragrance and is named *Enc. alata majus*. At one time, Belize exported large numbers of these species. The two varieties usually grow at the same locations and *Enc. alata majus* may be distinguished as the pseudobulbs that are three or four times the size of *Enc. alata.*

Encyclia aromatica

The first description of this specie listed the flowers as highly fragrant, greenish yellow with white striped purple lip. The years have added many different plants with the same type pseudobulbs, from green to purple colored sepals, petals and lips. They are exact duplicates in size and structure as the original *Enc. aromatica* but with many color combinations from browns, reddish to yellow greens. Today there could be up to 100 different varieties of *Enc. aromatica,* also known as *Enc. incumbens* and all will fill a room with perfume.

Encyclia cordigera

The two varieties are *rosea*, which is found in Guatemala and Panama, and the variety *randii*, which grows in great numbers in Costa Rica. Both varieties have 2" to 3" mahogany and green flowers, which bloom up to 15 flowers on an arching, stem. *Rosea* carries a spreading rose lip that can be from light rose-red to deep rose-red. *Randii,* however, is distinguished with a spreading white lip marked with red-rose stripes. Both varieties have proven to be good parents whose offspring qualify for award-type reds and various novelty intergenerics.

Encyclia boothiana

The "Dollar Orchid" once grew abundantly in the Florida Everglades. Some plants are still available from Belize. A very popular miniature species that has clusters of round flat pseudobulbs; the pert yellow blooms, barred with red stand erect on a 3"- 4" stem.

Enc. boothiana (Psh. boothi

Enc. fragrans (Psh. fragrans)

Encyclia adenocaule (nemorale)

Mexico contributes this very beautiful species to the orchid world. The glossy 10"-15" green leaves grow from ovate pseudobulbs that bear long stems with many rose pink flowers. Blooms are delightfully fragrant.

Enc. cochleata (Psh. cochleata)

Epidendrum ciliare

The spidery white flowers, stretching to 5" across with a fringed lip are still an all time favorite. As the flower ages, it turns greenish and then yellow. Usually seven flowers appear per stem.

Encyclia fragrans and radlata

Both species bloom on compact stems with 2" round, creamy flowers with spreading, shell-like, flat white, purple lined lips. *Enc. fragrans* has compressed, deep green pseudobulbs up to 8" tall and two long deep green leaves. *Enc. radiata* grows short, chubby, round very light green pseudobulbs and leaves of the same color. The "cockleshell" encyclias with non-resupinate (upside down) flowers as well as some other species, are now botanically placed in the genus, *Prosthechea (Psh.).*

Encyclia cochleata

The well-known cockleshell orchid has an upright, purple-black lip, leading many to also call this species "the black orchid". The size of the twisted, narrow, yellow-green petals and spreading black lips varies from small to large, according to the section of Central America in which the plants grow.

Epidendrum pseudepidendrum

The reed stem, leaves, and size are the same as *Epidendrum paniculatam*, which blooms pendulous yellow/green to pink 1" flowers. In the past, many growers sent money to exporters in Costa Rica for this very expensive and rare plant, only to find that it bloomed out *Epi. paniculatam*. The brilliant green flowers with 3" reflexed petals and wide, glowing orange, fringed lips still distinguish *Epi. pseudepidendrum* as a gem in any orchid collection. Happily, enterprising growers have raised populations from seed, erasing any doubt about authenticity, and making this formerly rare species much more widely available at reasonable prices.

Epi. stamfordianum

Epidendrum stamfordianum

The many fragrant yellow flowers, spotted with red and offset by a wide white to yellow lip, make a real show in early spring. Repotting can shock the plant and it may require a year to get the plant reestablished. However, once started the species can be easily grown into a showy specimen plant. *Epi. stamfordianum* has the unusual trait of flowering from the base of the mature growth, rather than the apex, much like *C. walkeriana*. This lends a spectacular nature to the display on large plants.

Encyclia vitellina

This is one of the few orange-red encyclias with the variety majus preferred. The plants have very small round pseudobulbs with long green leaves. A dozen or more 1½" flowers bloom on an 18" stem. *Enc.vitellina* hails from high elevations in Mexico and hence can be difficult to bloom in warmer climates. It also seems to prefer more shade than many of its warmer growing cousins. Now known botanically as *Prosthechea vitellina*.

Encyclia tampensis

A favorite with Florida orchidists as it was once found growing from Key West to the middle of Florida. Sassy, small greenish flowers with purple lips bloom abundantly on arching sprays. It can still occasionally be found in trees along rivers and in swamps. *Epi. magnoliae* can be found in cooler parts of Florida growing along with clumps of *Enc. tampensis.*

Epi. pseudepidendrum

Dendrobiums

Dendrobium Glinda Bibus

Den. formosum

While walking through the lush, tropical jungle in the lower Himalayas (which rise to over 25,000 feet and are covered with snow) we were startled at suddenly seeing brilliant yellow *Dendrobium* blooms covering the trees and mountainside like an umbrella. In other areas were plants on limbs of trees of *Dendrobium formosum* with large white blooms and buttercup eyes. This was a sight to behold.

Surprisingly, the plants were not growing in the lush dense trees or dark jungle areas. Orchids were growing on tree trunks and in the tops of trees where lots of sun and light could get to them. The trees were in open areas, some singularly in an open field. Dew in the morning and rains fed the exposed roots, and direct morning sun stimulated the growth and initiated the flowers. We realized that to adapt our growing conditions as near to nature as possible, orchids can be the easiest plants to grow and the hardest to kill.

One could use the words "stupendous, colossal or magnificent", and still not describe the many sensational *Dendrobium* hybrids. Think of the improved new "nobiles" that are extremely hardy and much easier to bloom than ever before. They grow and bloom well where it is hot as well as almost freezing. Plants produce hundreds of brilliant yellows, whites and pinks with contrasting dark colored throats.

There are dozens of new evergreen semi-terrestrial *Dendrobium* creations by the University of Hawaii that grow over 6' and produce multiple stems of long lasting brilliant flowers. These have been a boon to the international flower market and many acres of orchid farming have developed.   The newly developed dwarfs and semi-dwarf dendrobiums are perfect for interior decoration. Hundreds of thousands are commercially grown in 4" pots and available all year in bud and bloom.

It is not unusual today to see these evergreen dendrobiums blooming in pure whites, red lavenders or pinks, decorating offices, homes, restaurants and hotels. More and more, the blooming plants are seen on television programs and in home and garden magazines.

Dendrobiums are a varied genus of hundreds of species. Indeed, it is one of the largest and most diverse of all orchid genera. They are found from the tropics of New Guinea to the cool Himalayan Mountains and across the south Pacific area, providing a choice of varieties to please everybody. Over this large area the plants are growing in different heights, temperatures, and wet, as well as dry areas.

Dendrobiums have thin wiry roots that grow shallow and have the least extensive root system of all popularly grown orchids. The plants can bloom in a short time from seed and many begin blooming while still growing in a 2" pot. When potting, select a smaller pot than you use for other orchids and allow about 1/2" between the plant and the pot. Most orchid potting materials can be used; however, watering is different from most other plants. Always keep these orchids moist but use caution in keeping wet. Like most orchids, new roots and growth start in the spring and regular watering and fertilizing is needed during the following growing months. Many grow dendrobiums on slabs or in pots and in wood slat baskets, particularly the pendulous varieties. Some dendrobiums are robust growers and can reach exhibition sizes to bloom a shower of over 500 flowers.

Deciduous varieties are exemplified by species like *Dendrobium nobile*, *Den. pierardii* and *Den. superbum*, which are the most readily available and popular of this group. Plants grow either semi-erect or with pendulous pseudobulbs. New growth is covered with leaves during active growing months. Do not disturb pseudobulbs that are bare and have previously bloomed, as many dendro-biums will continue to bloom from old canes. Cut back the watering and eliminate fertilizing in the fall. The leaves will turn yellow and gradually drop off (this is painful to many growers) but is necessary to initiate bud formation. If watering is continued and leaves stay on the plants, it usually produces few flowers but it will grow keikis instead of buds. During the winter the plants enjoy temperatures down into the 40's, which enhances dormancy. Misting the plants and roots occasionally will prevent dehydration. Most dendrobiums thrive well when grown and treated the same as vandas - intense light, high humidity and regular fertilizing. In late winter the nodes around joints of the canes will begin swelling and develop clusters or spikes of gaily- colored, highly decorative flowers. Begin freely watering when you see bud formation begin.

Evergreen dendrobiums have accounted for the greatest progress. Plants retain glossy foliage all year and begin blooming in a relatively short time. Some plants have been known to bloom in two years. Plants begin producing spikes with many flowers from a relatively short cane. As a result evergreens are proving to add opportunities to pot plant as well as cut flower markets. Many valuable evergreen species were collected in Australia and New Guinea and were selected as parents of new hybrids. Antelope-type hybrids introduced many colors including yellows and greens with spur-shaped lips and pointed petals. Hobbyists and commercial orchid growers are attracted to these plants as the various hybrids will furnish blooms about every month in the year.

Den. biggibum var. compactum

Many free blooming ever-greens flower throughout the year. Most background breeding origi-nates from antelope-type species. Prior to the development of many evergreen hybrids the most popular variety was *Dendrobium phalaenop-sis* with large, round, flat flowers in colors of white, purple, and pink. These hybrids bloom in the fall and like a rest period after the plants have finished blooming. The *Dendrobium phalaenopsis* group was originally developed in the Hawaiian Islands. This species, originally found growing in Australia, has stout, slender, erect 12" to 36" pseudobulbs that pro-duce many 3" wide rose purple flowers. Different colors and shades of flowers were found blooming from pure white to deep rich purple with outstanding form. The species became the most important orchid in the development of hybrid "Den Phals." Dendrobiums gained pres-tige and popularity when growers in Hawaii developed new *Dendrobium*

phalaenopsis types. This created new beauty, as flowers are large and round; noted for size, shape and colors. Actually the different varieties of this widespread species, such as the whites, two-tones, and lavenders, were intercrossed many times to create today's beauties. Thus the creation of new ever-greens, standards as well as miniatures, is recognized as a great breakthrough in dendrobium hybridizing. Also these flowers are welcomed during crucial blooming months in fall through Christmas as well as *Dendrobium phalaenopsis* types.

Not to overlook many of the hundreds of *Dendrobium* species which individualize themselves in vibrant yellows, oranges to whites. Some of the best-known and popular species are: *Dendrobium chrysotoxum, Den. fimbriatum, Den. formosum, Den. aggregatum, Den. farmerii,* and *Den. draconis.* However, unlike in past years when wild-collected plants were inexpensive and easily available, growers may have to search to find some of these showy and worth-while species.

Most dendrobiums produce small plantlets or keikis on older stems devoid of leaves. They usually grow from a joint or upper part of the cane and aerial roots are developed in about 3 months. At this stage you can remove the keiki and pot in a 3" pot. They grow rapidly and sometimes bloom the first year. Also, after flowering, old canes can be cut between the nodes, dipped into a fungicide and placed on very porous soil such as sand, charcoal,

Den. Burana Emerald 'Natasha' HCC/AOS

or fine orchid potting material. Grow in heavy light and keep damp. Growths become active at the joint and develop a plantlet within a few weeks.

Dendrobium superbiens
Also originating in Australia, this orchid was a favorite with growers for many years before it was used extensively for hybridizing. The pseudobulbs grow from 1'-3' high and produce many 2" crimson purple flowers which show more substance than the flowers of *Dendrobium phalaenopsis* types. Challenged by the success of "Den Phal" hybrids, the University of Hawaii continued work to develop additional *Dendrobium* hybrids. Warm growing *Dendrobium* species were used which were found in New Guinea and Australia. They continued to grow and bloom all year and did not require a rest period. These evergreen types had been collected for many years but because the flowers were odd-shaped with narrow twisted long petals, they were not considered for hybridizing. When the first evergreen hybrid plants began blooming, they became recognized from Thailand,

Singapore to Hawaii. The flowers were smaller and did not have the form of *Dendrobium phalaenopsis* but the colors, numbers of flowers per stem, and more importantly, the vigorous plants bloomed throughout the year. Some of the evergreen species that have been important parents of hybrid dendrobiums are *Dendrobium stratiotes, Den. ionoglossum, Den. shulleri, Den. gouldii, Den. taurinum,* and *Den. veratrifolium.* A few of the first hybrids were Den. May Neal, Den. Jacquelyn Thomas, Den. Tomie and Den. Waipahu.

Den. aggregatum

stems can reach 6' long and are a beautiful sight, with 4" flowers singly or in pairs blooming from every node. The rich colored deep magenta rose flowers are famous for their powerful fragrance. Plants like a rest period after reaching terminal growth and usually drop all the leaves before blooming. A few plants that bloom pure white have been found.

Dendrobium aggregatum var. majus

This is one of the most popular species and imported plants are still occasionally available from India and Thailand. However, today, you will more often find divisions of select plants that have been in cultivation for some time and proven themselves as superior. Clumps of short pseudobulbs each with a single leaf produce a shower of round, flat, 1 1/2 " wide yellow flowers with a much darker yellow wide flat lip. There are many showy flowers on hanging stems. The plant is considered miniature and is reasonably priced. The variety jenkinsii is a smaller plant with darker yellow flowers. The more currently accepted name for *Den. aggregatum* is *Den. lindleyi.*

Dendrobium anosmum (D. superbum)

This fine species is known by the native Philippine exporters as *Den. anosmum* and by the Hawaiians as Hono Hono. The thick pendent

Dendrobium chrysotoxum

Club shaped, thick 6"-12" high pseudobulbs, make an attractive plant. The plant likes a rest period

Den. chrysotoxum

before it blooms in early spring. Many blooms form on a hanging or upright inflorescence from the nodes of the stem. The flowers are golden yellow with an attractive fringed orange lip. This species is known to bear blooms from the older stems also and is a real beauty.

Dendrobium densiflorum

Several dark green leaves growing from a 15" high stem that is also dark green and unusually four-sided characterize this species. Many

Den. secundum

orange-yellow flowers with a darker lip are growing dense on a drooping stem.

Dendrobium thrysiflorum

Identical to *Dendrobium densiflorum* except flowers are a white blushed pink with orange lip.

Dendrobium farmeri

The plants of this species grow only about 6" high but are exactly like *Den. densiflorum* with the exception of the blooms. The plants that grow in Nepal have pink blooms and a hairy yellow lip. The variety shipped

out of Thailand bloom white flowers with a deep yellow lip.

Dendrobium secundum

Many have been found growing in the Philippines and are known as the "toothbrush orchid". Round, brush-like pendulous stems with many deep rose flowers have attracted many admirers.

Dendrobium aphyllum (D. pierardii)

This popular species is vigorous growing and can grow quite large in pots or baskets that resemble a waterfall of flowers at the time it is in full bloom. The pencil-like 5'-6' canes need a rest period in early winter so plants can shed the leaves. In early spring, the white, rose, yellow and purple 2" flowers bloom in twos and threes from the nodes spaced 2" apart down the entire stem. Often blooms will come back year after year from the old stems.

Dendrobium loddigesii

To fully enjoy this orchid it should be grown to cover a fern basket or a large fern or cork slab. The creeping small pseudobulbs will bloom hundreds of 1 1/2" round, rose, orange, purple and white flowers with a fringed lip.

Den. densiflorum

Den. nobile

Dendrobium nobile

An all-time winter and spring favorite that was originally imported from India. 2"-3" flowers cover the 18" stems that bloom in twos and threes from each node. The blooms are white, heavily tipped reddish purple and the black crimson lip is bordered with white. Plants require a rest period when it reaches terminal growth in the fall. Withhold water and fertilizer, and keep in a cool area with low temperatures above 32. The plant will lose most of the leaves before initiating blooms. In Japan the Yamamoto family has done a superb hybridizing job over the past 30 years. Whites, yellows, pinks, red-purple flowering hybrids are now available. Over the past few years, the Dutch have entered the market with "nobiles" that are much freer-flowering and compact, if lacking the range of color of the more traditional Japanese types.

Dendrobium fimbriatum var. oculatum

Beautiful 4' upright pseudobulbs bear drooping stems with 20 or more deep orange flowers. The attractive wide lip has maroon "eyes" at the base of the heavily fringed lip.

Dendrobium formosum

In the late spring near Mt. Everest, this species covers the trees growing at the foot of the Himalayan Mountains of Nepal. It is breathtaking to see the flowers en masse and in the background the snowcapped mountaintop goes into the clouds. The 12"-18" stems have black hairs and 2"-5" pure white flowers that bloom from the top of the plant. A large yellow stained lip creates delightful contrast.

Dendrobium draconis

Similar to Den. formosum with the black hairy pseudobulbs, this orchid has pairs of 2" pure white flowers with red lips.

Dendrobium crumenatum

From 6" four-sided pseudobulbs, grow branching stems that can reach several feet. It is called the "Dove Orchid" because hundreds of white dove-shaped blooms cover the plant during the summer.

Den. crumenatum

Dendrobiums

Den. Adora Nishi 'H+R' AM/AOS

Den. Ise

Den. Mini Stripe x Mana Gold

Den. Gatton Sunray FCC/RHS

Dendrobiums

Den. Burana Stripe

Den. Quique Ramirez 'Karens Delight' AM/AOS

Den. Global Village

Den. Tropic Blue

Odontobrassia Kenneth Bivens

Oncidium - "The Dancing Lady"

Onc. Gower Ramsey

Out there is the dream of riches beyond comprehension. Everyone thinks of cashing in on one great deal of a lifetime. In late 1800, orchids were bringing unheard of prices, particularly for a new spectacular orchid discovery. Many were challenged to travel to all parts of the world and seek their fortunes by bringing back new orchids. England's control of countries like Ceylon and India offered convenient opportunities as there were jungles filled with orchids. There were regular merchant ships making frequent direct trips. This provided orchid collectors a better chance to reach England with plants in good condition.

An English explorer searched the mountains of Ceylon hoping for one major discovery, and at night was easily attracted to the famous beautiful Ceylon dancers. Continuing his search to Central America, he was spellbound when he came upon a mass of glistening, golden yellow, doll-like flowers gracefully moving with the wind. How beautiful and exotic, he thought, like the dancers of Ceylon. His discovery of oncidi-

ums was rewarding as he introduced an orchid as "The Dancing Lady", a symbol of the beautiful indigenous dancers of Ceylon (Sri Lanka).*

*From a menu in the Mountain Hotel in Kandy, S.L.

This is the most spectacular of the garden orchids! Truly what you mean when you say "exotic". It evokes the essence of every hour-of-the-day pleasure.

Oncidium orchids dominate the window, patio, garden, greenhouse or trees because the first plants bloom with up to a thousand blossoms at a time in great cloud-like masses of glorious color. Most of all you'll love the colors — primarily in glittering shades of yellow to bronze, white and pink, some

Onc. Sharry Baby

spotted with brown. Choose either the exquisite 1" - 3" blooms or the heavy 1/4" to 1" bloomers. Some oncidiums flower for up to three months. There are several hundred varieties - most plants are moderately priced.

The culture is easy—most varieties need moisture all the time. During active growth, plants will consume more water and fertilizer than cattleyas; however, oncidiums do best with a defined period of rest, generally during the winter or some time before and after flowering. Oncidiums have rather thin roots and overwatering is harmful. Well-drained orchid potting material is suitable; but oncidiums do best when underpotted.

Onc. lanceanum

Below are listed the favorite species and there may be other varieties or hybrid oncidiums you wish to grow.

Oncidium altissimum

This is one of the giants of the tribe. Bloom spikes can reach three to six feet or more with many branching scapes. Thousands of gold nugget flowers may be seen cascading from one plant. *Onc. altissimum* has a very extensive root system. Larger plants grow best if planted in slat baskets.

Oncidium maculatum

The best plants were originally found in Mexico and large numbers easily found their way into the United States. Plants grow 10" thin green leaves and the bloom spikes carry several 2" yellow-green, brown-blotched flowers with light yellow lips.

Oncidium crispum

This has been a very important stud plant and the 2 1/2 -3" ruffled flowers and lip have created many outstanding hybrids. The broad flowers are brownish, bordered yellow, and large expan¬sive lip is yellow spotted red. The unusual crisped flowers are responsible for its name. Twenty or more flowers bloom on branching spikes up to 4' high.

Oncidium varicosum

Another Brazilian *Oncidium* that, along with *Onc. crispum*, has helped to create an important variation on the classic "Dancing Lady" types. Most often seen as the Rogersii type, which has a very large and round pure yellow lip, *Onc. varicosum* displays its blooms on large, branching spikes of up to 40 or more flower when well grown. This species does best with a pronounced dry winter rest.

Oncidium lanceanum

Oncidium lanceanum has truly won its place among the most beautiful orchid species. For years large numbers of plants were gathered in the Caribbean Islands and South America and shipped all over the world. Today, we have seed-raised plants from the best of these. The showy flowers are 2" to 3" across with red spotted greenish yellow petals. The large spreading lip has been found from rose and purple colored to deep red and purple. The foliage is up to 20" long, mottled, medium green and mule ear shaped. The fragrant flowers bloom on stout upright 18" to 30" stems in generous numbers. The thick-leaved oncidiums known as "mule ears" are now botanically placed in the genus *Trichocentrum*. You will still often find them offered for sale as oncidiums.

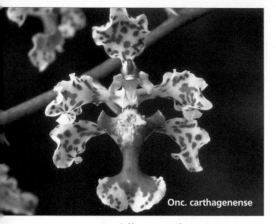

Onc. carthagenense

Oncidium carthagenese

This is a favorite orchid that is recommended to those who admire rose-colored flowers. Plants have large, thick, leathery dark green and often spotted leaves. Multitudes of one-inch flowers will bloom on up to 5' branching scapes.

Oncidium luridum

It was first famous as the beloved bee swarm orchid of the Florida Everglades. For years the Seminole Indians had a good income gathering specimen plants - some leaves reaching 24" long and 6" wide - for orchid collectors. As a result, the plants have all but vanished from the Everglades. The large mule ear leaves produce long arching spikes of cinnabar and yellow blossoms on branching stems. The odd-colored blooms are eye catching and when used in cross-pollinating they have produced some beautiful hybrids. *Oncidium carthagenese* and *Oncidium luridum* are both known as mule ear orchids.

Oncidium ampliatum

This unusual species is often called the turtle orchid. The round, dull green, mottled purplish red, wrinkled pseudobulbs resemble the top shell of a turtle. Many 11/2" brilliant yellow flowers are spotted red and have spreading white and canary yellow lips. Flowers bloom on arching branching spikes. The species is always a welcomed spring bloomer.

Oncidium kramerianum and Oncidium papilio

Both are known as butterfly orchids and botanically known as *Psychopsis*. The leaves and growths of both plants are alike but there is some small variance in the lip and petals. These are among the only oncidiums that produce solitary flowers. The plants, however, can produce many flower blooms sequentially on a long spike and usually when one finishes blooming another will bloom on the same spike extending the blooming period for several months. The plants are very compact and a spectacular specimen plant with dozens of flowers will be found growing in only a 6" pot. It does well with not too much water on the roots.

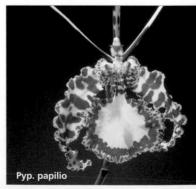

Pyp. papilio

Oncidium splendidum

They are very enjoyable and truly one of the favorite *Oncidium* species. The plants have leathery leaves and produce upright spikes with 2" buttercup yellow blooms on several branches. This orchid can be enjoyed for weeks in the spring as a pot plant or in bouquets. These plants are no longer being collected and shipped from Central America; so divisions or seed raised plants are the main sources of new material.

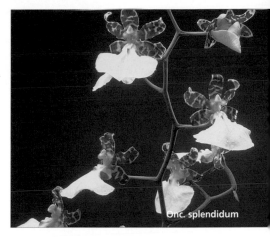

Onc. splendidum

Equitant (or miniature) oncidiums

Also known as tolumnias, these have rigid pointed leaves that grow in a characteristic fan shape. These novelty flowers are attractive and unusual because of their mammoth lip size in relation to the rest of the flower parts. The miniature plants bear flower

. Popoki 'orchidworks.com' HCC/AOS

stalks 12"-24" tall with sprays of 3/4" to 11/2" wide flowers. The best species commonly have yellow flowers, but pink, white and brown forms are found. No wonder the curiosity of growers increased when crosses from miniatures bloomed with rare and exotic colors - many uniquely spotted. Today increased breeding continues to produce amazing results in sizes and colors.

Tissue culture enables growers to enjoy the very best hybridizers can offer at prices that would once have not even bought an inferior hybrid. You can enjoy many different colors as plants are grown in 2" pots or mounted on logs. Their roots are fine and do not like to be kept wet. Equitant oncidiums are found in the Caribbean Islands, Central America and Brazil. The very wide and anchor-shaped lips have attracted growers for years. Most of the flowers are warm yellows and some have red spotted lips. The unusual number of large flowers in proportion to the small plants created much interest among hybridizers. Today hundreds of hybrids in colors of yellow, pink, red, orange, greenish and brown have earned awards. The species that hybridizers used to pioneer popular equitant hybrids are: *Onc. variegatum, Onc. pulchellum, Onc. triquetrum, Onc. desertorum, Onc. urophyllum, Onc. henekenii,* and *Onc. lemonianum.*

Bllra. Marfitch

And they are easy to grow in the home or on the patio in warmer areas. Most appreciate more light than *Phalaenopsis*, though somewhat less than *Cattleya* types, and prefer to be evenly moist. Like dendrobiums, these will do best if slightly underpotted, so remember to pot for the bottom (the root mass) and not the top. Mature plants can have multiple branching spikes on each lead bulb, with a display lasting many weeks in perfection. While there are types requiring more coolness, those generally available will be from warmer growing blood. Don't be afraid to give these a try!

Thisever-popular group of genera is being crossed to create some of the most unusual colors and shapes. They are commonly called "intergenerics." The genera that make up this exciting group include *Brassia, Miltonia, Odontoglossum, Oncidium*, and many others. When combined, they create such intergenerics as *Aliceara, Bakerara, Brassidium, Burregeara, Colmanara, Degarmoara, Maclellanara, Miltonidium, Odontocidium, Vuylstekeara,* and *Wilsonara*. This group is truly the "success story" of the latter part of the twentieth century, second only to *Phalaenopsis* in widespread variety and appeal. Initially, these were considered cool growers and not satisfactory for mass marketing. However, as hybridizers have worked their magic, and tissue culture has become perfected for this type, we are seeing the true range of this awesome group. While *Phalaenopsis* are generally similar in shape and size, varying in color and patterning, this group can range from true miniatures to majestic display plants bearing literally hundreds of brightly colored blooms. Perhaps in no other group is a wider array of colors, sizes, shapes and patterns seen than in the Oncidium Alliance intergenerics.

Brassia
Known for their long narrow sepals and petals and the lip is shaped like the body of a spider. The plants have been most valuable to hybridizers and are responsible for several of the most beautiful intergeneric hybrids. The specie flowers are green, yellow, to brown and are heavily spotted. Brassias are often mistaken for oncidiums, as the plants are very similar in color and shape. *Brassia caudata, Brs. maculata, Brs. longissima, Brs. gireoudiana,* and *Brs. verrucosa* are the most important species. The species plants are almost impossible to find and some growers have started selfing and meristemming in order to reproduce seedlings.

Brs. Rex 'Sa

Milt. spectabilis

Odontoglossum
A cool, high elevation genus, which require 45 °- 60° temperatures to grow well. The usually unbranched flowering spike comes from the base of a mature growth and produces medium size blooms in two ranks along the arching stem. Odontoglossums are grown extensively in Europe and cooler areas in America.

Miltonia
The beauty and shape justifies this genus to be known as the "Pansy Orchids". From narrow pseudobulbs, attractive thin, light green leaves, they produce from the inner basal leaf and arching *Phalaenopsis* type spray of up to 20 medium flat flowers. *Miltonia spectabilis, regnellii, flavescens,* and *clowesii* can be grown in warmer climates with cattleya growing conditions. The majority and more spectacu-lar varieties require night temperatures in the 50's and not over 80° in the daytime. These miltonias are generally "cool growers" because many species come from high elevation especially the Columbian species. Today, this type is most commonly known by the new name *Miltoniopsis*. These are generally difficult to grow under home conditions anywhere by the cooler, northern areas. More and more intergenerics are becoming available today indicating great possibilities in future hybridizing, particularly as it is a member of the *Odontoglossum* tribe, which includes *Oncidium, Brassia,* and *Odontoglossum.*

Odm. Rustee

Brsa. Orange Delight

Mtssa. Royal Robe 'Jerry's Pick' HCC/AOS

Oncidium

Mtssa. Jungle Cat 'African Queen' FCC/AOS

Colm. Wildcat

Dgmra. Kramer Island 'Everglades' AM/AOS

Milt. Brasilia 'Everglades' HCC/AOS

Phalaenopsis Elizabeth Hayden

Some of the earliest plant explorers found pink and white *Phalaenopsis* species growing on trees in the forests of Assam through Burma, the Philippines, Malaysia, and Indonesia. Their sometimes thousands of flowers on arching sprays, gracefully moving in the sunlight, reminded these early explorers of flights of moths.

Today the attractive thick leaved, glossy green plants with their arching sprays of flowers that continue to bloom for months have become the most popular orchid houseplant. The multitude of blooms is a spectacle to behold and, more important, the flowers can last longer than almost any other orchid (from 5-10 flowers open at one time with buds that continue to bloom for 3 months). As an added "bonus," when the flowers are gone and the stem is still green, if the stem is cut just above the joint ("node") where the first flower bloomed, another branching stem will grow and, like magic, flowers will continue to appear - sometimes for as long as a year. Or, an offset or keiki will form from the joint of the spike when flowers have died. Also available today is a chemical paste that can be applied to the joints, which will encourage new plant growth. When the aerial plants have grown roots several inches long, remove and plant in a pot.

Phalaenopsis are the easiest to grow and blooming size plants are reasonably priced. You can grow them and you can afford them. You will also be surprised when you have grown a spectacularly beautiful plant with many blooms. You may feel like the office beauty who was regaling her bored companions with the tale of her adventures on the previous night. "This feller," she said, "took me up to his apartment and showed me a closet that contained at least fifteen absolutely perfect mink coats. "And what do you know," she said, "he gave me one of them." "What did you have to do?" asked the skeptic in the audience. "Just shorten the sleeves," she said.

Much like thoroughbred horses, in a little over 30 years hybridizers began to produce highly prized *Phalaenopsis* plants with startlingly brilliant blooms. Complex and varied new hybrids continue to thrill growers with immense (up to 6"!) blooms, comprised of a triangle of petals with a spade lip. Most have long stems with multitudes of dazzling flowers - a spectrum of colors including whites, light and deep pinks, yellows, newly created reds, deep stripes, spotted, colored lips and many autumn colored combinations. *Phalaenopsis violacea* crosses bloom on short compact stems, very close to base of the plant. These plants bloom for months and have an individual place to enjoy.

The tallest and heaviest flowering plants are grown with good sunlight, frequent watering and fertilizing and temperatures above 60-65 degrees. Some compare growing *Phalaenopsis* to African Violets, as the care is similar. However, you want to take caution with watering that the plant is not kept saturated. Be sure your potting material is moist when fertilizing. *Phalaenopsis* pots need good drainage. However, they may require more frequent watering than other orchid varieties. This is when you realize *Phalaenopsis* do not have pseudobulbs for storage tanks, as do other orchids. This is when you realize *Phalaenopsis* do not have pseudobulbs for storage tanks, as do other orchids.

These handsome plants are known as "low light" orchids and will grow in about any situation with bright indirect sunlight. *Phalaenopsis* will tolerate heavy sunlight but if sunlight is too intense it will burn the leaves. *Phalaenopsis* grow well throughout the year by bright windows, in the basement, or anywhere there is adequate light, moisture, heat and movement of air. Where air is dry, plants will benefit by rubbing a wet cloth over the leaves or misting frequently. This is an ideal houseplant to grow as it will grow and bloom in more shade than most other orchids. Almost any window can be used to successfully grow phalaenopsis—lightly shaded south, east, or west - but a north-facing window will almost never provide sufficient light to bloom the plants.

Take advantage of Mother Nature's prolific life-giving goodness when potting your *Phalaenopsis* Select an orchid clay pot with slits at the bottom, a plastic pot with enough holes at bottom, or wood slat basket. Place coarse materials such as rocks, shell, broken crock or any material for perfect drainage and fill up to 1/3 of pot. Many potting materials are used today although the old adage that the material available in your area at cheapest prices can be adequate if you adapt your cultural practices no longer holds. While redwood or fir bark, tree fern, charcoal, or cypress chips are usually available, it is always advisable to see what other materials are used successfully in your area and purchase them from a reliable source. If possible, obtain your potting materials from folks who know how orchids grow. Suppliers such as Better-Gro use their products and know they work. New potting materials regularly appear on the market, and there is no harm in experimenting with a plant or two. Remember! Experiment with a couple of plants that are growing well but are not your favorites, just in case the new medium is not useful under your conditions.

Phalaenopsis originated in tropical areas where they are often found growing on rocks or limbs of trees. Therefore, you may find the roots of your plant rambling over the top of the pot seeking air, light and moisture. Some growers are having extra success by placing chunks of Canadian peat in the potting material. If so, extra caution must be taken concerning frequency of watering. It was once an axiom that windowsill or indoor growing was enhanced if potted plants were set on a tray of rock and water. While we now know that the humidity is not appreciably raised, it is a convenient way to catch the water draining from your plants after watering, and so can still be a useful trick. It is best to repot *Phalaenopsis* at least every two years in late spring immediately after plant has completed blooming. If repotting is completed by June, the plants can become reestablished before the next blooming period. Choose a pot that will accommodate root—do not overpot. A good axiom to remember is "pot for the bottom not for the top." Trim off dead roots, wind remaining roots gently into pot, place plant 1/2" below rim of top of pot, add potting material and pack around the roots. The best time to water plants is in the morning with care to keep water out of the crown or center of the plant. Stake the blooming spikes to keep the flowers arching upright. *Phalaenopsis* plants continue to flower for several months. When the first flower opens, more buds continue to form on the top of the spike. As mentioned above, many hybrids will form secondary spikes of flowers after the first sprays of flowers have faded. Often, plants will continue blooming for as long as a year. The stem is cut just below the first joint that bloomed the first flower. Additional spikes of flowers may continue to come from the lower stem joints.

This constantly charming plant is highly recommended for beginners and loved by hobbyists for its ease of growing and blooming rewarding flowers of such beauty. There are many known different *Phalaenopsis* species, which have been discovered since the first were found in the 1700's. A related genus known as *Doritis*

Phal. amabilis

has added pink coloration with vigorous growth habits. These are known when crossed as *Doritaenopsis*.

Phalaenopsis will banish all your fear and disappointment in growing orchids and are destined to become your favorite plants. A handful of countries have furnished the over 50 species of *Phalaenopsis*, which we enjoy today and are responsible for the many spectacular hybrids available. A few *Phalaenopsis* species may be found in more than one country. The following are the species that have been most important in giving the many colors and sizes.

Phal. Brother Orange Runabout

Phalaenopsis amabilis

The king of the jungles is one of the parents of most large flowers that are enjoyed today. Several varieties of 3" to 5" white flowers bloom on tall arching stems are also found in Java, Amboina, and Queensland. The yellow lip, spotted red has proven important. Some hybridizers are backcrossing with the species to improve strength, texture, color and vigor.

Phalaenopsis aphrodite

White flowers, flushed with pink that has a pink and yellow lip.

Phalaenopsis intermedia

This species has broad white petals and a three-lobed white lip spotted red with the side and front lobes of reddish-purple.

Phalaenopsis leucorrhoda

A species that has medium-large white flowers and white lip, spotted red-purple and stained yellow.

Phalaenopsis sanderiana

No species has been more important to hybridizers than the spectacular *Phal. sanderiana*. Three-foot spikes, some branching, large pink flowers with yellow-red spotted lip are the ideal features for a good pink parent.

Phal. schilleriana

Phalaenopsis schilleriana

Equally important as a top pink species, they have many large rose-purple flowers cascading on a 4' branching scape. The flowers are 3" wide and have been crossed with large whites to produce larger size pinks, blooming by the hundreds on branching inflorescences.

Phalaenopsis stuartiana

These very attractive plants bear branching sprays of 2 1/2" white flowers. The inner half of the sepals may be yellow, spotted red. The lip is yellow and purple spotted. Malaya, New Guinea.

Phalaenopsis amboinensis

A variety of new autumn colored flowers have excited many growers from plants with *Phal. amboinensis* background. The small yellow flowers with cinnamon-brown bars have been responsible for very interesting colors when crossed with pink or white *Phalaenopsis*.

Phalaenopsis leuddemanniana

A wide number of hybrids have come from this species as several color forms have been collected. The cream to yellow flowers along with those barred brown are important in producing yellow hybrids. Some species are rose-purple and others are striped pink. The plants are known to bloom all year in the Philippines.

Phalaenopsis mariae

These plants have yellow flowers, which are barred. The lip is purple. The stems are branching which enhances the beauty of the arching blooming sprays.

Phalaenopsis violacea

The flowers occur in two forms: Bornean and Malayan. 2" to 3", flowers bloom from zigzag spikes. The Borneo form is pale green, often with waved margins, bright violet-purple at the base with purple and yellow lip. The Malayan form has smaller, pale flowers with more uni-form rose purple color. The Bornean form is now considered a separate species, *Phal. bellina*.

Phal. lueddemanniana

Phalaenopsis gigantea

The largest *Phalaenopsis* plant and distinguished by magnificent green leaves that can reach several feet long and 12" wide. The plant is noted for the plant size rather than flower size. The flower is medium-size, creamy white and is spotted brown with a reddish lip.

Phalaenopsis cornu-cervi

Burma and Java also furnished these small yellow green flowers, barred with brown and with a white lip.

Doritis pulcherrima var. esmeralda

This species originates in Thailand. The plant grows 6-8" hard leaves; thrives in higher temperatures and sunlight than most *Phalaenopsis*; and produces growths from the base that can be cut from mother plant and planted in another pot. Many one-inch flowers continue to open for months on 30" stems. The flowers are light pink-purple and some with dark flowers have been collected. The variety *buyssoniana* blooms larger, flat flowers. These species have become outstanding as the parents of many exhibition pink *Phalaenopsis* hybrids.

Dtps. Brother Pungoteague Creek

Miniatures

Many orchidists have recently become fans of miniature orchids. It may be that the beauty of new *Cattleya* miniatures and *Oncidium* equitants was the first attraction to these small prolific plants. However, other advantages are space savers, large number of blooms, and the fact that you can have an orchid blooming every month in a small space. Miniatures are great for orchid growers who feel they have no more space for additional plants. They see the possibility of squeezing just a few more small plants into their collection.

Following are species largely used to create miniature *Phalaenopsis*.

Phal. equestris

Phalaenopsis equestris

A white blushed with light pink or purple. The plant grows several spikes with 1" flowers and is usually in bloom all year.

Phalaenopsis lindenii

Flowers are 1 1/2" wide, very pretty and are important for the pink color and purple stripes. Several other species such as *Phal. cornu-cervi* are also being used in miniature hybridizing.

Phal. mannii

Phalaenopsis mannii

Long-lasting small yellow flowers with brown markings that grow on a branching stem. The flowers were used extensively in hybridizing to develop large yellow *Phalaenopsis*. The plants are grown over a large area in India in low altitudes of the Himalayan Mountains.

Phal. Brother Fortune Sara 'Rogers' HCC/AOS

Phal. Fangtastic John 'Sedona Bright Smile' AM/AOS

Phalaenopsis

Phal. Joy Spring Canary 'Nancy' HCC/AOS

Phal. Plantation Beau 'Diane' AM/AOS

Phal. Golden Peoker 'BL' HCC/AOS

Phal. Homer P. Norton 'Glowing Ember' HCC/AOS

Phalaenopsis

Phal. Brother Supersonic

Dtps. Brother Pungoteague Creek

Vascostylis Kaleidoscope 'KG's Blue Adagio' HCC/AOS

V. Robert's Delight 'Torblue'

We were dazzled as we walked into the lobby of the Oriental Hotel in Bangkok, Thailand, and were spellbound to see an 8' island arrangement of orchids. There were long stems of huge vandas in a rainbow of different shades, dendrobiums, yellow *Oncidium* sprays, accented with *Aranda*, and red *Renanthera*. Instantly we realized that the decorative value of these elegant orchids would be recognized internationally and would be used in florist shops for the most elegant bouquets.

What is a *Vanda*? First and foremost, it is a magnificent plant that can be grown with great ease and is a pleasing addition to any orchid collection. It is a genus that is possible to bloom in the north and with great results in the south. And, more importantly, newly developed ever-blooming varieties are being introduced that can give you all shades of color the year round. Vandas are beautiful and graceful plants that can produce 30 or more symmetrical leaves, alternating along a central stem that can be in constant flower.

Today, the "super orchid" *Vanda* produces more colors than any other orchid and is particularly noted for sapphire blues and ruby reds. Over 15, 1" -7", flat flowers can bloom from an arching or erect stem. Pick your own colors as vandas can offer every color in the rainbow—velvet blues, pinks, greens, whites and since the first cross with ascocentrums reds, yellows, orange and salmons have been added to the nearly limitless palette.

What are the "Beauty Secrets" in growing vandas? Vandas require lots of sun, humidity and very frequent watering and fertilizing. The plants are heavy feeders, requiring more frequent watering and fertilizing than cattleyas. Some southern growers water every day - frequent misting of leaves and roots is excellent. Vandas never stop growing and may need watering twice a week even in the winter. A good step is to suspend plant with a wire hanger near the roof of green-house or where the plant can enjoy good air] circulation. *Vanda* roots need more movement of air than any other orchid. Plants cannot tolerate staying continually wet at the roots. Grow vandas in 70% or more light with temperatures always above 65-75°. Many Floridians grow spectacular vandas around their swimming pools.

Aer. lawrenciae

The Vanda Alliance

Four-Pollinia Group
Arachnis, Vandopsis, Pomatocalpa, Trichoglottis, Sarcanthus, Renanthera, Thrixspermum

Two-Pollinia Group
Vanda, Luisia, Phalaenopsis, Sarcochilus, Aerides

Vandas are grown well in both pots and slat baskets as the plants have large, heavy, fleshy roots that are difficult to contain in a pot. Plants do not like to be disturbed or repotted - new roots are not easily replaced from a repotted plant. When a plant has overgrown a slat basket, place entire basket, roots and plant into a larger basket. Rather than cutting or breaking the long aerial roots during repotting or re-basketing, soak them thoroughly to make them pliable and wind them into a circle that will fit into the new pot or basket.

Semi-terete and some varieties of strap leafed vandas can grow very tall and may become a problem. You can grow additional plants of the same vanda by cutting the top of the plant off. Once you have determined the size cutting you wish to take off, try to go down toward the base of the plant and cut below joints with one or more aerial roots. Apply fungicide to the cut area. This will prevent stem rot. Plant the cutting in a wood slat basket or pot. The plant from which you removed cutting should send out side shoots in a few weeks.

The most striking feature in the genus *Vanda* is the great range of color within the different species, possibly surpassing every other genus of cultivated orchids. Vandas lack only true red, found in the allied genus *Renanthera*. Almost every other color is found in the genus *Vanda*. Other properties that make the flowers useful and desirable as decorative plants are the attractive quantity and long lasting quality of the flowers - some last for over 3 months. Flowers are used for corsages, cut flower arrangements as well as use of the flowering plants themselves.

The three horticultural types of vandas are:

Strap Leaf—Strap leafed varieties have flat leathery leaves and are the majority of species and hybrids grown. These include the ascocentrums.

Terete Leaf—Terete vandas have stiff pencil-shaped leaves and are famous as the most popular flowers for leis.

Semi-terete Leaf—Semi-teretes are

V. sanderiana

X V. teres. Recognition must be given to this famous hybrid, which has produced the greatest number of commercial flowers. Millions of blooms are given away at store openings and promotions. The flowers are used by thousands of restaurants as a garnish on plates the same as fruits and vegetables. Many hotels place a bloom on the pillow on the beds for guests. Airlines that fly the Pacific include blooms on individual serving trays. Blooms are still

hybrids with terete species in the background. Plants require almost full sun to bloom and the flowers do not have the flat form and large size as most strap leafed varieties.

Vanda species that have been used to produce most of the hybrids are *sanderiana, coerulea, dearei, luzonica,* and *tricolor.*

Until recently, 95% of the *Vanda* hybrids had *Vanda (Euanthe) sanderiana* as a parent, predominantly the blues. However, many other species have been put into use in recent years, fueling great expansion in breeding, bringing additional colors, size and beauty.

used in floral arrangements as well as corsages. *Vanda* Miss Joaquim flowers have accounted for the first orchid received by millions. The lovely 2 1/2 " - 3 " flowers are very popular in leis on the tropical islands in the Pacific and halfway around the world to Sri Lanka where V. Miss Joaquims are grown commercially on hundreds of acres of land. Stakes or wire supports long rows of plants, and the plants grow over 12' tall. Flowers are harvested daily but still the supply does not meet the demand. Many companies use individual *Dendrobium phalaenopsis* blooms to substitute for vandas. The terete vandas are often placed in the separate genus, *Papilionanthe.*

Terete Vanda

These are tall, slender, vine-like plants with forked pencil-like leaves, and require heavy to full light to bloom. The species originated in Burma and is popular for the ease in growing and blooming. One of the first hybrids developed and grown around the world was *Vanda* Miss Agnes Joaquim. The parents were *V. hookeriana*

Asctm. garayi

Asctm. ampullaceum

Ascocentrum

An increasingly popular genus that is grown by those that like the dwarf plants, and for their brilliantly colored small flowers. The results of the crossing of the yellow *Ascocentrum miniatum* with a large strap leafed vanda produced fantastic colored medium-sized blooms. Instantly a revolution occurred among orchid growers and opened a popular trend toward growing vanda hybrids. The intergeneric cross of *Vanda* X *Ascocentrum* was named *Ascocenda*. Reds, oranges, yellows, violets and new shades of flowers in greater number per stem, on shorter, more compact and frequent flowering *Ascocenda* plants, have brought the "icing on the cake" to orchidists.

Arachnis

It is known as the Scorpion Orchid; the curved petals represent the claws and the top sepal the tail of a scorpion. This species is a climbing type orchid and will grow to more than 15' high. There are over 10 varieties that produce spotted, barred, yellow, brown and rose flowers. The plants grow in full sun in tropical countries and are grown in large numbers for cut flowers.

Aerides

They are very similar to vandas with dark green leaves that are not as stiff as vandas. The species vary greatly in size; some grow to a considerable height while others remain dwarf. The flowers are waxy, scented, good sized and borne on pendant stems. The lips are spur-shaped and curve upwards. The most popular varieties are *A. odorata* (a tall growing plant that will branch and create a massive plant); *A. quinque-vulnerum* (white flowers, tipped with purple, and purple spotted); *A. multi-flora* (leaves grow very close together on a compact short plant that blooms rose-purple flowers).

Aer. multiflora

Renanthera

It is famous as the parent of red *vanda* hybrids, as well as stunning display plants in and of itself. Vanda-like plants grow tall and produce branching stems with many flowers that last for months. There are three commonly seen varieties; *Ren. storiei* blooms 3' long stems of dark orange-crimson flowers;

Ren. imschootiana is a shorter growing variety but very important as it blooms scarlet red flowers; *Ren. monachica* also grows short and produces yellow or orange flowers with red spots.

Rhynchostylis

There are three well-known species: *Rhy. gigantea, Rhy. retusa* and *Rhy. coelestis*. The leaves are thicker than Vandas, grow close together on large stems, and can grow 12"-15" tall. Pot *Rhynchostylis* in very well drained orchid potting material and/or lump charcoal. A better growing job can be done if the orchid is planted in a wood slat basket. The bloom spike is thickly covered with 3⁄4"-1" flowers and is known as the "Fox Tail Orchid". The plant is well known for its fragrance. Like vandas, *Rhynchostylis* bloom from the base of the leaves and plants 10"-12" tall are known to have as many as 12 blooming spikes at one time.

Rhy. gigantea 'Banjong' AM/AOS

Rhynchostylis gigantea
Often has the largest flowers that are 1" wide, fragrant, white and heavily spotted lavender-pink with solid colored lip. Several years ago solid maroon red and pure white varieties were discovered and shipped from Thailand. All three varieties are widely available. Plants usually bloom in November and December. The inflorescences are pendulous.

Rhynchostylis retusa
Flower spikes reach 2' long with flowers 3/4" diameter. Lavender-pink spotted flowers and lavender-pink lip. It is a spring blooming orchid that flowers at Easter and Mother's Day. The flower stems are pendulous and blooms fragrant.

Rhynchostylis coelestis
Blooms during the summer. Flowers are white, tipped blue with same color lip. Plants from an area of the Philippines bloom a very delicate purple-blue color. Of the three species, only *coelestis* blooms on upright stems.

Aerdv. Bold Beauty 'Susanna' AM/AOS

Neo. falcata

Ascda. Laksi

Ascda. Thai Pagoda

Ascda. Mote's Burning Sands 'Redland Toast' AM/AOS

V. Golamco's Blue Magic 'Electric Shock'

V. Mote's Buttercup' AM/AOS

V. Wirat Sky Blue' AM/AOS

Vanda teresS

Phaius tankervillae

The Phaius Tribe

The main feature of these orchids is that they grow best in rich, well-drained soil.

Phaius

Two reasons to grow *Phaius*: very easy to grow and bloom, and the lovely flowers last for weeks. *Phaius* were first introduced in Europe in 1778 and they are as easy to grow as any houseplant. *Phaius* are excellent foliage plants with wide 12" long leaves that have a glossy, rich green color. The flowers are quite showy with an odd combination of reddish brown, yellow and white colors. The 12"-24" erect stem will bloom up to 50 flowers. The 4" blooms have a tubular throat. Looking into the throat, the white pollen and star resembles a hooded nun praying, thus it is called "Nun's Orchid" or the "Veiled Nun" (use some imagination). *Phaius* can easily be grown to become a specimen plant in just a few years.

With 12 to 25 blooming spikes at one time, it makes a spectacular show. However, plants are normally divided and repotted every two years. The plants grow well in shade or heavy light and should be fertilized every month. New plants can also be grown from the old bloom spikes. When plants have finished flowering, cut the spike into sections with at least two joints. Place on top of soil and keep moist or plant cutting with at least one joint under the soil.

While there are over 20 *Phaius* species, *Phaius tankervilleae* is the choicest. It is at home in windows, outdoors or in greenhouses where temperatures are above 50°. Enjoy the beautiful plant; give it plenty of water and fertilizer and many flowers will bloom from this handsome plant.

Phaius tankervilleae

Cal. vestita

Calanthe (means "beautiful flower")

Pot and grow calanthes the same way that *Phaius* are treated. There are up to 50 species and all are terrestrial. The deciduous species grow with long pseudobulbs and leaves. The leaves fall off before or at time of blooming. The evergreen species produce leaves from rhizomes. The foliage is among the most beautiful of all plants and is a welcome addition to your home or greenhouse. The flowers, 20 or more per stem, will remain in bloom for over 2 months.

Ble. striata

Bletilla

This may be the first orchid grown by most people. The ease of growing and the beauty of the flowers created the interest to seek other orchid plants. Thousands of the dormant bulbs are sold every year in stores along with gladiolus, dahlias, etc. *Bletilla striata* is known as the "Hardy Orchid" as it can be grown and treated the same as daffodils. The bulbs are usually planted during the dormant period. The plants grow palm-like foliage and bloom rose to amethyst purple flowers. If left growing in a pot they will produce additional growths and flowers the following year. *Bletilla striata* is found in Vietnam, South China and Japan. Today Japan grows and exports these bulbs each year. A solid white variety is also available.

Lus. discolor

The Physurus Tribe — "Jewel Orchids"

Handsome Jewel Orchids are appropriately named for their exquisitely marked foliage, which is so varied in shades and unusual markings; it is difficult to fully describe their beauty. Each variety individualizes its plant with distinctly colored leaves and prominent, contrasting veining. The leaves are a beautiful sheen from green, dark red, silver or purple and veined, mottled or blushed in shades of gold, silver, red or yellow. Many white flowers bloom on an upright spike. The flowers are often used in small arrangements and bouquets, as they are dainty and last for two weeks. There are still changes being made in the names of the species. However, the following are known: *Macodes, Ludisia (discolor), Anoectochilus, Goodyera, Dossinia,* and *Erythrodes.* While many have found the plants difficult to grow, use a very porous, well-drained humus soil; keep damp but never wet; and grow in medium shade. The stems are fleshy with succulent leaves and should easily grow along with begonias.

Vl. planifolia

Vanilla

Yearly, millions of people are amazed when they visit Walt Disney Epcot Center and see the fabulous, huge vegetables and plants of tomorrow. The "people mover" takes you around the greenhouse and you see enormous squash, cabbage and other oversize vegetables. Among the plants growing in a section are *Vanilla* vines. Yes, pure vanilla extract is made from beans that grow on an orchid plant. The most widely grown species are *V. planifolia* and *V. pompona*. There is a leafless variety, *V. barbellata*, that grows in the hammocks of South Florida. The leaves on the *Vanilla* vines are thick and green; greenish yellow flowers are produced successively from the leaf axils. The vines are known to grow great lengths and it is not unusual to see a vine climbing to the top of a greenhouse. The flowers open and die in a day and in order to grow a *Vanilla* bean, pollination must be done by the grower. Few flowers are ever pollinated in nature and you cannot depend on bees to do the job.

V. teres var. aureo-labia

Catasetum intergerrimum

Cyrt. punctatum

After flowering, the plants drop their leaves and require a decided rest period of several months. It is a very fast grower and needs lots of water. The plants have short, fat and usually sharp pointed pseudobulbs. The roots are large and are heavy feeders. While there are many different species that bloom flowers of various colors, *Catasetum pileatum* has proven to be the really handsome one. The ivory white, goodsized flowers of *Catasetum pileatum* have a wide oyster shell lip and are used extensively in hybridizing.

Cyrtopodium

Cyrtopodium punctatum is a native of Florida, which makes it very special to American hobbyists. It has been found in Mexico and south into South America. The species of this genus are all very large growers and require a lot of space in a greenhouse. The slightly curved pseudobulbs grow up to 3' long with 24" green leaves. From the base of the long pointed bulbs, a branching stem, 5' or longer, blooms hundreds of bright yellow, shaded green, spotted red flowers. It is a real spectacular sight when it blooms.

Catasetum

Often known as the puzzle orchid because they may have male, female, or bisexual flowers on the same plant. The flowers have horns and the wind or an insect can trigger the pollen. The plant shoots the pollen and it can be scary to brush a bench of flowers and feel the pollen peppering over the body like small bullets. Catasetums are warm growing orchids that require heavy light.

Ctsm. pileatum

Cycnoches

This is a very beautiful and enjoyable orchid known as the "Swan Orchid." *Cycnoches chlorochilon* is the most outstanding species and was exported from Costa Rica. This species has the same growing requirements as Catasetums and the long thick, round stout bulbs will disintegrate rapidly unless they are kept bone dry after blooming. There are several *Cycnoches* species including *Cyc. egertonianum*, which is known as the Monkey Orchid. These plants also originate in Costa Rica.

Angcm. Veitchii (eburneum x sesquipedale)

Angraecum

A member of the *Vanda* tribe and it is mostly grown today by orchid specialists. The plants look very much like a strap leaf *Vanda* with closely spaced, wide leaves growing almost symmetrically on the stems. The most beautiful species come from the islands of Madagascar. Charles

Cyc. herrenhusanum

Darwin's work with *Angraecum sesquipedale* added to his fame. The flowers are 5" star shaped white

with a 14" spur. Mr. Darwin established the theory that a moth with a long elephant-like snout would go into the spur to pick up the nectar. People laughed at Mr. Darwin, but after his death such a moth was found. *Angraecum* species are growing in the hottest parts of the world and require temperatures over 55° for the best results. Additional plants can be grown by cutting off the off-shoots that frequently grow from the base of a blooming size plant. *Angcm. eburneum* plants grow very tall, 6' and over, and the arching spikes bear many 3" greenish white flowers. Each flower has a 3"-5" spur. *Angcm. distichum* is a miniature specie that grows short 3"-6" stems with narrow overlapping pencil point size leaves. The small white flowers are produced from the axils of the leaves. *Angraecum* plants always become a conversation piece when it blooms stems of unusually star-shaped hard, glossy flowers from deep green leaved plants. The blooms last for weeks and are often sweetly scented at night.

Paphiopedilum

Usually known as the "Lady Slipper" orchid. New hybrids are most attractive and demand a high

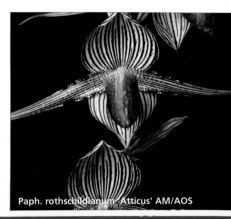

Paph. rothschildianum 'Atticus' AM/AOS

price. Most popular warm growing varieties grow with mottled leaves and the most popular is *Paphiopedilum* Maudiae. "Bulldog" types have green leaves and require temperatures from 50 °- 65°. This is a terrestrial genus with hairy roots, which never should dry completely. *Paphiopedilum* flowers are among the longest lasting of all orchid blooms and come in an astonishing range of colors, patterns, spots and shapes. Because they are shade-loving plants (in general), they are also among the best and easiest orchids to grow in the home. An added attraction is their foliage, which can be as brightly patterned as any Jewel Orchid, giving year round appeal. While the often bizarrely shaped and colored blooms are definitely an acquired taste, the long-lasting and waxy flowers add architectural line and interest to home décor. More and more retailers are finding that it is to their advantage to have these on hand for their more discerning clients.

Cym. Something Fabulous

Cymbidium

More *Cymbidium* flowers are used in corsages than any other orchid in the world. A spray of cymbidiums can bloom with up to 50 large flowers (though 15 - 20 is more common) and last up to eight weeks after cutting. With the exception of parts of Florida and most of Hawaii, cymbidiums will grow well in greenhouses and outdoors in many areas. The plants grow very large which can be a problem with indoor space. Many space saving miniatures are becoming popular even though the flowers are much smaller. The few warm growing species are much less common, but they, and especially their hybrids, are becoming increasingly popular in warmer area such as Florida and the Gulf Coast, where they will make a fine addition to patio décor.

Cymbidiums have been known to stand near freezing temperatures and as high as 110° for a short time. Many areas of the Pacific southwest grow cymbidiums well in open gardens. Continuously high temperatures found in many areas weaken cymbidiums and unless there is a good cooling system provided, the plants will not flower. *Cymbidium* species are found largely in mountain areas, which extends up to 10,000 feet elevation and the temperature averages up to 80°.

Lc. Gold Digger 'Orchid Jungle' HCC/AOS

Orchid plants with superior qualities are submitted for awards and judged by American Orchid Society trained judges. A minimum of 75 points is necessary for a plant to qualify for an award. The awards and number of points are as follows:

HCC/AOS	Highly Commended Certificate	75-79 points
AM/AOS	Award of Merit	80-89.5 points
FCC/AOS	First Class Certificate	90 or more points
CHM/AOS	Certificate of Horticultural Merit – Odd or rare species with horticulturally desirable qualities	
CBR/AOS	Certificate of Botanical Recognition – New, or never-before exhibited species	
CCM/AOS	Exhibition plant grown to special size, beauty and excellence of culture; only award given to grower and not to plant, 80-90 points.	
CCE/AOS	Same as CCM but scoring 90 points or higher.	

Awarded orchid plants are superior in many ways as brilliance of coloring, larger size, strong plants and exceptionally fine shape. While this is an indication of the quality of the plant, most orchids are never entered for judging. Many unjudged plants have proven to have exceptional qualities and are very fine parents.

To enjoy growing orchids, it is best for each individual to be governed by their own choice of beauty.

1) Why won't my orchids rebloom?

The most common reason is insufficient light. All orchids need good quality, bright light to bloom. Of course, some need more than others, and it is often simply a matter of moving the plants a few inches, or feet, to brighter light. Always remember to allow the plants to adjust to higher light by moving them gradually, a portion at a time. Also, orchids tend to be seasonal, so maybe you're just being impatient. Has it been a year yet?

2) My plants have black spots on the leaves, what is this?

If your plant is in heavy light or direct sun during the hottest times of the day, it is sunburn. Burn is caused not by light, but by the heat generated by the light. Plants can "burn" simply from heat stress. That is why your plant "melted" in the car, even though you parked it in the shade.

3) I grow my orchids in the house and I always have the air conditioning on, and my plants don't seem healthy, what's wrong?

Air conditioning is extremely drying, as is the general home environment. Humidity is necessary and this can be created in a number of ways, all discussed earlier in the book.

4) If it is necessary to remove dead roots when repotting, how do I know when roots are dead?

Healthy orchid roots are white and firm, dead ones are often brown and soft, or "rotten" looking.

5) I cannot seem to get rid of scale, what should I do?

One treatment of anything will not rid your plants of pests. It often takes two, three or even four treatments, at seven to ten day intervals, of a nurseryman recommended product to kill all the various life stages of the pest.

6) What insecticide should I use on my plants?

First identify your pest, then use a product specified for its control. Orchids are more hardy thank you think, to be on the safe side, if it can be used on a tender plant such as a fern, it ok for your orchid. Today, the most commonly used insecticides for orchids are light horticultural oils and/or soap-based products.

7) What are some of the pests I should look for?

The most common are scale, mealy bugs, spider mites, and aphids. And remember, these pests can come from your other household plants. By far the most commonly seen pest today is the mealybug, which is a white, waxy creature about the size of a small ladybug. Because of the their waxy coating they are particularly hard to get rid of, and often need several treatments. A wetting agent may sometimes be added to the pesticide solution to help penetrate the waxy coating.

8) My plant looks off color, yellow, and weak, I probably over-watered it, what should I do?

Shake it out of the pot, check the roots for signs of root rot. If the roots appear rotten, remove and allow the plant to dry out slightly. Repot into the smallest possible container (sized appropriate to the remaining root mass) and keep the medium on the dry side, while providing increased humidity in the atmosphere.

9) Light must be my problem; I just purchased a light meter, what now?

Vandas, dendrobiums and cattleyas take between 2000-3000 foot-candles; miltonias and oncidium types between 1500-2000, were low light plants like phalaenopsis and paphiopedilum grow well around 1000 foot-candles. However, it is far better to learn to judge appropriate light without resorting to a light meter. This is especially important, as "light" is not an absolute, objective term. The amounts of light different orchids will need/take at different seasons is highly dependent on the area in which you are growing i.e. north vs. south. Far better it to learn to assess light conditions based on your observations at different times of the day, and the way in which the plants respond. For example, dark green, soft foliage is an indicator of low light, while hard, yellow, stunted foliage indicates too much light and the attendant stress.

10) What should I look for when contemplating the purchase of an orchid?

One of the most important features of a quality orchid plant is the label of the nursery that produced it. Look for general plant health, the most important aspect of which can be seen in the way the plant sits in the pot. Is it firm in the pot and well rooted, or does it appear to have just been potted into a larger pot to give the appearance of value? If buying a flowering plant, never buy a plant with flowers open to the tip of the spike, instead, look for buds to come to lengthen your enjoyment.

A Potpourri of Orchid Facts

Mltnps. phalaenops

- Physicians once believed that plants which resembled human organs could be used for drugs for treating the organs. The reputation of orchids was very popular as aphrodisiacs, and particularly for regulating fertility.

- Orchid plants are still useful in many crafts and trades. Gum from *Ansellia gigantea* is used to cement stones and wood together.

- Dried stems of dendrobiums are the materials used for weaving pocketbooks in Malaysia.

- The Tasaday of the Philippines dries *Trichoglottis wenzeii* for G-strings.

- Horns for communication are made from *Schomburgkia tibicinis* in Central America.

- *Schomburgkia thompsoniana* pseudobulbs are shaped for smoking pipes in the Cayman Islands.

- *Oncidium cebolleta* are eaten by natives of Mexico because of their "miraculous" hallucinogenic effects.

- Catasetums and cyrtopodiums are used to produce glue in South America.

- *Bletilla striata* is used extensively in China and Japan as a drug to treat several ailments. *Dendrobium nobile* stems, when dried, are also extensively used as a drug to treat a vast range of ailments.

- *Vanda tessellata* roots and leaves from Ceylon are regarded specifically for rheumatism. Varieties of *Vanilla* leaves and stems are mashed by Magaysious (a tribe in Sri Lanka) for hair tonic.

- *Cypripedium acaule* is known as a love tonic.

- *Vanilla* is the most productive orchid today that is still being used throughout the world commercially.

American Orchid Society

AMERICAN
ORCHID
SOCIETY

For more than eight decades, the American Orchid Society (AOS) — a nonprofit scientific and horticultural organization — has extended the knowledge, production, use, preservation, perpetuation and appreciation of orchids. Today, more than 22,000 members and 400 affiliated societies worldwide enjoy the benefits of being associated with the AOS, the world's largest specialty horticultural organization.

The principal benefit of belonging to the AOS is access to a wealth of information geared to helping you enjoy this most wonderful and fulfilling of passions — growing orchids! From its colorful, award-winning monthly magazine, Orchids, to member-access to botanical gardens and arboreta around the country, to one of the top horticultural Web sites in the world (www.aos.org), the AOS delivers innumerable educational and informational resources to its members.

In addition to including a subscription to Orchids, membership also includes a free copy of Your First Orchids, a 10-percent discount on items purchased in the Orchid Emporium giftshop, free admission to the AOS Visitors Center and Botanical Garden (in Delray Beach, Florida), and much more!

If orchids turn your head and grab your attention, check out the AOS. Growing orchids is, you will find, an intense affliction. It is never fatal, however; indeed, the hobby is entirely pleasant and immensely rewarding!

American Orchid Society
16700 AOS Lane
Delray Beach, Florida 33446-4351
Tel 561-404-2000 Fax 561-404-2100
E-mail TheAOS@aos.org
Web site www.aos.org

Growing orchids successfully is so easy...

"GROWING ORCHIDS IS FUN
takes away the confusion and
mystery of growing orchids"

Tom MacCubbin,
Host of Better Lawns & Gardens radio

TOPICS OF INTEREST

Phalaenopsis

Vanda

Dendrobium

- Potting
- Dividing
- Breeding
- Orchid Identification
- Troubleshooting

This guide takes a step-by-step approach
to proper potting mixes, light, water, and
fertilization of a wide variety of orchids.
Written for beginners, hobbyists, and
orchidists as an adventure in the joy of
growing orchids.

Also included are 150 orchid color
photographs and illustrations.

0 79925 05347 7

BETTER-GRO
We Know Orchids - We Grow Orchids